THE CULTURAL DEVELOPMENT OF LABOUR

Also by Paul Corrigan

*SCHOOLING THE SMASH STREET KIDS

Also by Paul Joyce, Paul Corrigan and Mike Hayes

*STRIKING OUT: Trade Unionism in Social Work

*Published by Macmillan

The Cultural Development of Labour

Paul Corrigan
Education Research Officer, Labour Party

Mike Hayes
*Senior Lecturer in School of Social Research
Polytechnic of North London*

and

Paul Joyce
*Chief Training Officer
Islington Council*

MACMILLAN

First published 1991

Published by
MACMILLAN ACADEMIC AND PROFESSIONAL LTD
Houndmills, Basingstoke, Hampshire RG21 2XS
and London
Companies and representatives
throughout the world

Edited and typeset by Povey/Edmondson
Okehampton and Rochdale, England

Printed in Hong Kong

British Library Cataloguing in Publication Data
Corrigan, Paul 1948–
The cultural development of labour.
1. Great Britain. Employment. Social aspects
I. Title   II. Hayes, Mike 1940–   Joyce, Paul 1952–
306.360941
ISBN 0-333-52402-0 (hardcover)
ISBN 0-333-52403-9 (paperback)

Contents

Preface

The labour market is in crisis. It enters the 1990s suffering from severe structural faults. The simple belief that labour will find its own price – that people will come into the labour force for the rewards on offer, and that these rewards in some way represent a sufficiently attractive price to draw people into labour in the right numbers for the right sorts of work – no longer holds. It is this very simplicity, this naturalness of the hidden hand of the market, that we believe is so open to question.

In Part I of this book we demonstrate the way in which that crisis goes beyond any simplistic view of a skills mismatch, or a small scale cultural problem about work. The problem is endemic and concerns long term breakdowns in the way in which training fails to meet the needs of the country, either intellectually or economically. This failure is not just a matter of some puzzles about the structures of the nation's organisation of training, rather it reflects a long-term lack of care with regard to investment in labour.

The issue of inequalities in the labour force, where women and black people are systematically excluded from certain sorts of opportunities and forced into other ones, also represents a considerable economic loss. It may be claimed that these inequalities have become recognised, that the race relations legislation and the Equal Opportunities Commission have been set up to tackle them. Yet their very lack of success demonstrates not simply a lack of legal might in tackling these problems, but more significantly, it demonstrates the powerful effects of social and cultural inequalities created primarily outside the world of work and regenerated in that world. The economic waste of gender imbalances in the labour market may be realised within that labour market, but their cause and construction is to be found in the wider social inequalities of gender in the home and in wider society.

Part II underlines the different policies that have been followed in an attempt to shore up that labour market. We demonstrate that for the most part these policies are ineffective and on occasions manage to make the situation considerably worse.

In Part III we outline the theoretical reasons why the labour market broke down in the early 1990s and explain the interventionist policies that are necessary to reconstruct the relationship between labour and society.

PAUL CORRIGAN
MIKE HAYES
PAUL JOYCE

Part I
Problems in the Labour Market

Concern over the working of the labour market in Britain was always evident. In recent years it has centred on unemployment and on rigidities in the market's operations. This is not surprising given adult unemployment in excess of 3 million (according to Government figures) during the mid 1980s, and given the hope of Government that a more flexible market would lead to increased competitiveness and thus more jobs. By the end of the 1980s, however, three specific problems had also moved into the centre of public debate: attitudes to employment, the state of training, and employment discrimination against women, ethnic minorities, older people and others. This was no doubt a reflection of the falling rate of unemployment, the emergence of skill shortages, and the belated realisation that employers were going to find themselves facing shortages of young workers as a result of demographic trends.

Part I explores these problems, which were to some extent made more prominent by the specific circumstances of the late 1980s, but which nevertheless had a more fundamental importance in relation to long term developments in Britain.

1 Why Don't People Want to Work?

The labour market in Britain is in crisis and, at its heart, the crisis is one coming out of the cultural nature of labour. It is this issue that we will raise in this first chapter, where we demonstrate the interaction between the economic and the social sides of labour.

We start with the way in which the present crisis interacts with British culture as a whole. For most people, for much of their lives the experience of someone in their household going out to work provides the material necessities of life. For most of these households the period Monday to Friday of nearly every week is dominated by going out to work. And when the annual holiday is taken or when the family come together for religious holidays, the main experience is characterised by *not* having to go to work.

As we shall show throughout this book, there are sharp gender differences contained in these experiences. Many women, even though they are in work, will have their household defined by their male partner's work. Many women who are not in paid labour but are engaged in child care and other domestic labour will have their household defined not as a childcare household but as social class 1 to 5 depending on what their male partner does. Our argument is based in part upon the tensions between the world of work and the world of home, but the power of these male work based definitions still dominate many women's lives.

Similarly for those people who are 'out of work'; their major experience is defined by a 'lack' of work – by being 'un'employed. Their social security benefit as their prime source of income will be defined in a similar way; their social esteem and standing will also be defined as that deficiency of work.

In later life older people are seen as retired. This means that they may spend 20 years living an entirely different life style, characterised not by the single fact that they are not doing the paid work that they did for many years before, but by taking part in very different activities as a retired miner, car worker, shop worker, textile worker, health worker, etc.

From a young age children are expected to be able to label 'what they want to be when they grow up', not with a human characteristic such as 'kind', 'strong' or 'loving' but with the label of a job. I will be a computer operator, nursery nurse or teacher when I have grown up – and they are defined by that occupational label even at that early stage.

The dominance of the world of paid work is underlined *both* in its importance as providing money and, for many, its importance in providing meaning and definition in life not only for the person in work but for their household and for their future household.

WHY THE STRESS ON CULTURE?

We make this string of what may appear to be obvious points because most analyses of the labour market fail to discuss the social and cultural nature of that market at all. They portray the economic relationship of going out to work as if it takes place in a cultural and social world entirely separated from that of the world of home. Because working for money is such a necessity, it is somehow taken away from the world of culture. For this world is seen much more clearly as one where people construct social relationships, make choices and decide activities. It is as if social culture is allowed because it is somehow not necessary, whereas the lack of choice about having to engage in paid work makes the use of the word culture a lot less meaningful.

Of course people can recognise the importance of occupational culture, can link the way in which people work with the way in which they live. But such studies as *Coal is Our Life* (Dennis, Henriques and Slaughter, 1969), a brilliant 1950s book on the way in which working in the pit dominates and creates the social world of the pit village, is now essentially an historical or anthropological text.

Such experiences of working class culture seem to belong in the historical theme park, rather than in the complexity of social and economic life in the 1990s. Such a relationship between work and home was always a minority one. It could only work where the physical proximity of one particular form of work totally dominated one locality to the complete exclusion of all others. Even then there were problems; for in such a pit village there could be no source of female paid labour since that would have constructed a very different labour market experience. Where there was no alternative, a single dominant relationship between the world of home and the world of work could be understood and delineated as a 'culture'. Under those circumstances the home-work culture could be reproduced every weekend and evening and, most significantly, every generation. Young men would know that most of them would go down the pit – unless they escaped from the locality; young women would, after an interval, have further families of miners – unless they escaped from the locality.

Generations of homes of pit workers recreated the future generation of pit workers not only through the tied cottage system of housing, but through a sort of 'tied culture'. That was what there was.

In a mine-culture where there was very little choice, it is possible to see the way in which culture actually creates a labour market and a labour market comes back and creates a culture. We can see that if we want to understand why people went down the pit, then we had to understand the culture. Yet for much of the world then, and for nearly the whole of the world now, that simple empirical one-for-one relationship does not hold. Under those circumstances it appears that culture does not seem to matter. It is our contention that it does, but it is much more varied and difficult to trace.

In the final section of the book we emphasise the different way in which we see culture actually producing labour. Here we demonstrate how some of the recent emphases of social and political strategies have helped to shape a culture which devalues the experiences of work. Of course this has not been their intention: Government has stressed the absolute importance of working for a living. But their economics and their social theory are such that they have helped to create something which they were hoping to stop.

We would stress that morally, and in a general social sense, we do not disagree with the power of the world of work in defining life. We believe that labour is a very important aspect of life, and plays a vital human role in both creating individuals and in creating society. We do believe, though, that recent political, social and cultural emphases on work have created a particularly deformed emphasis which has essentially affected the culture of British people in relation to the world of work. In this chapter we explore how that cultural experience has been created and transmitted.

We believe that this cultural deformation of the way in which labour has been experienced has been created not only by the way in which the Government has treated the workforce when in the world of work, but also how public policy has totally failed to appreciate the way in which labour is produced *culturally* by a world outside of the world of work – by the family, by leisure, by education and by popular culture itself.

In short, a society which fails to appreciate the importance of social and economic investment in the world outside work, which fails to see how this world has to produce the worker and create or return them to the world anxious and longing to work, will in the end produce people who will be impoverished workers.

In Chapter 3 we point out how the social experience of gender, ethnicity and other inequalities play a significant role in the corruption of the labour market. In these cases, our argument goes, the social relationships outside the world of work are *vital* in understanding how that labour market works.

INVESTING IN LABOUR LOSES JOBS

There are two major issues about the way in which labour is viewed culturally, and our analysis of them will run through this book.

Firstly, in recent years employers and Government alike have stressed that the only important *productive* activity in society takes place when workers are at their benches, lathes, desks or sales counters. When they are apart from that moment of production then they are not only failing to produce wealth but they represent a *cost* to those people and moments when wealth is being made. Given this view of economics it is then essential to increase the amount of time of the 'productive' moment, and decrease the time of the 'unproductive and costly' moments. The latter would in a clear and direct sense involve all time spent training, all time at lunch hours, all time involved in child care, all time involved with colleagues at work discussing work (unless that was in your job description as a job manager), and in fact, *all* such time that is not actually spent doing the job.

This dominant cultural approach to labour argues that if we as a society spend time and resources doing all of these things, it simply increases the costs of business and decreases our competitiveness. Sometimes these moments represent a double cost. At one and the same time it may be not only a moment *not* producing, but also a moment spending resources and therefore acting as a drag on the moments that are producing.

In late 1989 this was most succinctly expressed by the Government's powerful rejection of the European Commission's Social Charter. As put to the Council of Ministers in December 1989, and as expected to be carried out throughout Europe, there are a series of necessary investments in labour itself. Investments in training, in benefits, in child care, in health and safety – all constructed not simply as abstract social and political rights for workers, but as necessary economic interventions in making labour more productive. For the European Community this plan is a necessary part of economic growth.

For the British Conservative Government it is a cost.

As outlined in Chapter 2, a society which has the British attitude to investing in its workforce will inevitably end up with much too little training.

We are suggesting that more than a decade of such an approach to labour has transcended the field of 'social and economic policy' and has now become a major cultural factor in the way that British society *as a whole* experiences labour and experiences investment in that labour as a 'cost' and not an investment. We are suggesting in this book that this long term cultural experience leads society to see labour as something which is itself devalued. If it is 'wrong' and costly and a waste to invest in labour, then, as a part of society and as an aspect of economic production, labour is literally devalued. It is this devaluation which plays a major role in creating the present problems *not* simply at the level of a social and economic policy, but also at the level of popular culture and everyday life. The dignity and importance of labour is devalued in ordinary people's lives.

I ONLY DO IT FOR THE MONEY

The second major issue which has affected the way in which labour is viewed culturally is the importance of payment. In a capitalist society being paid is one of the major experiences linked to work. For many people it is the dominant experience of work and for quite a few it represents the only reason for working. This is especially so given the day by day experience of alienation that takes place within the experience of work. As we shall see, the long term relationship between payment and work is one that has been built up not only through the world of work, but also through the social security system. Such a system has been constructed to 'police' the labour market and to ensure that those people who do not go out to work to receive their remuneration are punished. Money and work have been firmly linked for many generations.

Such a link, however, has not removed the ability for work to provide other positive experiences for workers. Most industrial sociology points out that work involves other important aspects. Companionship and friendship is gained at work; the experience of working together collectively at an enterprise takes place at most places of work; despite the alienation workers also experience some aspects of fulfilment in the work that they do – work provides them with achievements in construction and whilst there are few who would unequivocally see their work as making their life, there are many who see some aspects of accomplishment in what they carry out.

All of this takes place alongside payment. Whilst workers would stress the importance of payment, they do so because there is no other way that most people can achieve their material needs than linking work and payment. As we shall explore in the next section, Conservative Governments since 1979 have underlined the important nature of payment for work. People go out to work, and work hard, or harder, in order to get more money. Whilst Thatcherism may describe the role of the entrepreneur as gathering more and more social roles around them; entrepreneurs are those persons who through their activities go out and make the world in their competitive image. It is they who more than any other are responsible for revitalising arts, sport, ideas and future. Without their thrusting and restless competitiveness society becomes lax and useless.

But there is no similar cultural role for the worker. They have to work hard to earn their money. They must apply themselves to the tasks worked out by the entrepreneur and the market. Their niche is created by those forces. Consequently their work, in and for itself, is irrelevant. If the entrepreneur cannot make it it happen and if the market does not want it, however beautiful or self-fulfilling that work is, it is actually and literally useless. It is without use if it cannot be bought and sold.

Between 1979 and 1982 unemployment increased to over 3 million. Time and again it was made clear that the work that people had been doing in a variety of industries was now no longer of any use because the product could not be sold. Skills that had been carefully constructed and reconstructed over many generations were declared to be 'useless' because they could not be sold. The effect of this particular cause of unemployment has been profound, not simply by creating large numbers of unemployed people, but by demonstrating that labour and skill can be discarded so easily. The intrinsic nature of mining coal, smelting steel or working in a car components factory is demonstrated to have no worth at all. Why should people feel that their next job, or the one after that, requires any skill at all?

Consequently, within this world view, work for the worker is *only* the means to an end – the earning of money. Culturally this has always been a strong theme running through society – now it has become much more dominant and is for a great many more people culturally exclusive. If the only point of working is to earn money to live, then why not try to earn that money some other way? Under those circumstances labour is once more culturally devalued as an activity in its own right. Sure, most people will work in order to earn, but this becomes much more the reason why they are doing it.

These then are the cultural consequences of this dual devaluation and corruption of the role of labour. If it is wasteful to invest in the production and reproduction of labour, then millions of people begin to feel that it is not an important activity. If the only point of doing work is to earn money and everything else is dismissed with cynical abandon, then again people may think that it is not worth doing.

CULTURE AND CONTRACT

The Thatcher Government set out to change the economic culture of the country and to stress the importance of rewards for effort. We outlined these policies above because we believe they have been specifically aimed at the culture of working people – to demonstrate the importance of work and the wastefulness of non-work. Whilst we believe that there have been some considerable unintended consequences for this strategic attempt to change culture, it is important to note that the culture has been seen to be an important site for intervention. For labour market policy is usually described in such a way that it seems as though the market for labour takes place with no more regard for the nature of the commodity than it would be if we were describing the market in coffee.

The labour market in economic terms is viewed simply as that – a market. The commodity of labour is bought and sold at a price, the same as any other commodity. Just as some commodities gain a higher price because they are more favoured or are rare, such as Jamaican Blue Mountain coffee, some labour is better favoured and paid for than others. Coffee has no culture, no needs, no self-consciousness in this market place; in the best of all possible free market worlds the same would be said of people. When viewed as a collectivity, labour should behave as any other commodity and obey the market. Just as coffee has no responsibility for the way in which the market goes –

whether it is prized or whether it is dumped as useless – the same goes for labour. It can take no collective responsibility for its price or its uselessness.

However, the theory goes, when viewed as an individual in the market place, the coffee bean still has no responsibility whereas individual workers do. As individuals they engage in a contractual relationship in which they agree to be sold for that particular amount for that particular time. Their *individual* responsibility is all powerful in this contract. Laws, rules and whole social policies are constructed to make that individual responsibility take precedence. Thus if a coffee bean fails to sell, it is not the coffee bean's fault; if workers do not sell their labour power, however, it is their fault and they must act more 'intensively' and more 'effectively' in order to be sold (Employment Department, 1988, p.57). The failure of the labour market to engage them is not a market failure but is their failure – their individual failure, their personal failure – and it is explained as such. If they behaved better and looked harder, or groomed themselves better or asked for less money, or didn't worry about their children's care, then the market would be engaged and the relationship would be fulfilled.

This may seem an idiosyncratic, philosophical point to make but it goes to the very heart of our argument and to the political response of Government to the labour market.

Whilst the market has no responsibility to provide jobs, the individual has responsibility to find one. Whilst society must not take that responsibility and intervene in the labour market, individuals must, and if they do not, social and economic pressures will reinforce that responsibility on them.

The reinforcement of this individual responsibility is the cornerstone of political interventions in the labour market. Throughout Section 2 we will demonstrate that Government policy after Government policy has, through education and the social security system stressed the political and economic necessity to engage with the market. Here we are underlining the moral and cultural attempt to do the same thing.

If there are jobs and if people are not taking them up the fault is theirs. If they do take up jobs and then the market changes and the jobs are no longer necessary, they are sacked, but the fault is not that of the market. Indeed time and again the Thatcher Government blamed the workers for the loss of those jobs. In this way a policy for the labour market becomes culturally devolved on individuals in that market. It is up to them to make sure they are employable, in the right place, with the right qualifications, with the right child care, and all of their home arrangements conducted in such a way as to make their commitment to the labour market possible. If any of these things do not happen, then it is the individual's fault and not the market's or the Government's.

Our argument is that this policy of pure individual responsibility is not simply morally wrong but economically so. The labour market in British society in the 1990s is a Byzantine and complex one. It cannot operate with a single notion of a buyer and a seller of a commodity since the nature of that commodity is transformed on a regular basis. Someone who has spent 15 years within the market category of a 'steel worker' is not going to easily understand that the market category of 'receptionist' is also a category of labour. They may well say, rightly or wrongly, that it is not proper work. They may believe, rightly or wrongly, that they would not be able to successfully transfer the commodity of steelworker to that of receptionist.

Younger persons about to try and engage with the market may feel that they want to enhance their part of the market commodity called labour with qualifications for taking their labour to market in 20 years time. They will not know what such an enhancement is like. A woman outside of the labour market and wanting to enter it may well only see her possible ability to engage with that market through their past experiences of inequalities and quite wrongly judge the position in which she could enter the market. Similarly an older person who had spent 30 years engaged in one particular trade may quite wrongly feel there is no possible position for them in the 'modern market'.

Placing the total responsibility for the smooth running of the labour market on millions of individuals making even more millions of decisions, provides those individuals with an impossible burden of knowledge. In the examples we have outlined in the paragraph above many people will make the wrong decision and many other people will decide that the labour market cannot be entered into. It is too complex and has changed too much. If it is our personal responsibility, then it may well be the case that we will make decisions based not upon possibilities of the future but on experiences of the past. As such, a labour market left to the difficulties of individual responsibility is much more likely to place itself in a previous decade than in the decade in advance.

2 The Training Gap

INTRODUCTION

By the end of the 1980s it was universally agreed that there was a national training problem. A serious gap existed between the level and extent of the training which was being carried out and the training which was needed for a labour force in a dynamic, successful economy.

The Government said it, in the 1988 White Paper *Employment for the 1990s*. 'The fact is that in spite of many improvements we are not, even now, training enough of the kinds of people we need' (Employment Department, 1988, p.28).

Business leaders said it. For example, in early 1989 the CBI's Director-General not only identified people as the country's key source of competitive advantage, not only argued that investment was the key for business to meet the challenges facing it, but also said that investment in people needed to be increased. He wrote:

> Members of the Confederation of British Industry (CBI) see investment as the key to maintaining the momentum of economic recovery in Britain. Although our level of investment has increased over the last few years it is still well behind that of West Germany, Japan, and the United States. If British business is to be competitive with those countries investment in plant, building, research and development and, most importantly, people will need to be increased substantially above present record levels. (Banham, 1989, p.4)

The British trade union movement said it as well. The TUC summed it up as follows:

> But in one crucial area, Britain lags behind all these other economies. We are relatively untrained, and relatively unskilled....
>
> These shortcomings are expressed as relative because Britain now trains more people for longer than we have done since the war, despite the decline of apprenticeships in specific sectors. But we have fallen behind our competitors comparatively because they have done so much more than us. We are failing to meet the tasks of a late twentieth century economy. (TUC, 1989, pp.3–4)

Complaints about Britain's system of industrial training have been heard for thirty years. Alarm was raised about its part in Britain's economic downfall. There was the undeniable problem of skill shortages. 'Again and again during the 1940s, 1950s, and early 1960s, British industrial expansion came up against a series of bottlenecks caused by shortages of skilled manpower' (Shonfield, 1965, pp.117–18).

Skill shortages continued throughout the 1970s. At the end of 1973 for instance, the CBI's Industrial Trends Survey found that one-half of manufacturing firms were expecting shortages of skilled labour to act as a constraint on output (Eastwood, 1976, p.7).

A study of the UK engineering industry in the 1970s suggested that employers saw the problem stemming from Britain's failure to produce the skilled workers for them to recruit on the labour market:

> At the companies visited, management were invited to give their views as to whether the shortages they perceived were primarily due to difficulties of recruitment, retention, or inadequate labour utilisation. The great majority said they experienced a recruitment problem, that the skilled workers were not on the market, and that apprentices were not coming forward.... There is a long tradition within the industry of going into the market and endeavouring to find skilled workers. (Eastwood, 1976, p.9)

Empirical research, which we will consider shortly, reveals a major difference between Britain and advanced capitalist economies in the vocational qualifications of workforces. The research indicates that the low level of training and skill in Britain is responsible for appallingly low productivity levels and very unenviable competitive positions for British industries.

The system of vocational training in Britain, which appears quite different from those of West Germany, France, Japan and the United States, is defective not only from the point of view of the relatively small numbers of people gaining vocational qualifications, but also in the nature of the competences and skills which result. In short, the system produces too few qualified people and those that do receive qualifications are ill-prepared for working in a dynamic, modern economy in which computers, and modern technology generally, are necessary for high quality and high productivity.

The role of the Government emerges as crucial to British attempts to confront the contradictions in the vocational training system. In the

1980s the Government intervened massively in Britain's training system, but a major question remains about the extent to which that intervention shifted the national training culture, or whether it has merely been a cosmetic operation that has left the major contradictions untouched. It will be seen that there is much evidence that the nature of the Government's interventions has done nothing to close the training gap. Despite large expenditure on training, the actions have not been correctly targetted, and a major opportunity for the state to put the organisation of training on the right track has been missed. Much of what has been achieved represents a 'counterfeiting' of training, in which low levels of specific work competence are being certified as the 'genuine article', but do not measure up to the requisite skills needed for a modern knowledge-based economy.

VOCATIONAL QUALIFICATIONS

It is frequently claimed that vocational qualifications are a rarity in Britain. Despite the difficulties in making accurate and valid international comparisons, there is evidence that this general suspicion is well justified.

A careful comparison of the vocational training of engineering workforces in Britain, West Germany and France, three countries with very similar populations, showed that Britain lagged far behind in the production of craftsmen in 1985–6 (Prais, 1988, p.81). Whereas Germany produced 120 000 qualified craftsmen, and France produced 92 000, the number qualifying in Britain was only 35 000. Most (27 000) of those who qualified in Britain during 1985–6 took the City and Guilds examinations at Part 2 (Craftsmen) level, with the remainder consisting of people taking BTEC National Certificate examinations who did not go on to take the Higher Certicate.

One result of the relatively poor volume of qualified craftsmen trained in Britain is the difference it creates in the distributions of qualified personnel within industries. Whilst Britain produces reasonable numbers of technicians and more highly qualified staff, these are 'supported' by a relatively small base of qualified craftsmen:

> Both the Germans and the French have twice as many qualifying each year as craftsmen as they have qualifying as technicians or with university degrees in engineering: whereas in Britain... the number qualifying as craftsmen is less than the numbers qualifying at higher levels. (Prais, 1988, p.82)

As we will see later, factory comparisons suggest that British industry relies very heavily on unqualified supervisors, as well as on unqualified production workers. Qualified craftsmen provide an important source of personnel for supervisory cadres in West Germany, providing for supervision which is technically competent, in addition to any organisational skills they may possess.

An even more shocking comparison is provided by the retail sectors of Britain, Germany and France. The volume of vocational training for retail occupations in 1986 varied enormously; whilst 1650 people obtained qualifications in Britain, the comparable number in France was 14 500 and in West Germany was nearly 100 000 (Jarvis and Prais, 1989, p.60 and 67). The impact of this variation in training activity could be seen in the density of qualified staff in retailing occupations. In 1982, 24 per cent of all French employees in retailing occupations had either the Certificat d'aptitude professionnelle (CAP) or the higher level qualification known as the Brevet d'enseignement professionel (BEP). In contrast, in 1984, 3 per cent of British employees in retailing occupations had the BTEC National qualification or a City and Guilds certificate (ibid., p.60). In West Germany and France qualified retail staff are very common, whereas in Britain they were, in the 1980s, a rarity.

WHY TRAINING MATTERS

In a series of recent case studies the importance of training to economic performance has been strongly demonstrated. In one industry after another it has emerged that high quality and popular products are produced by workforces who are well trained, highly skilled and have advanced equipment which they are able to use to manufacture, flexibly, what is required by modern markets. Furthermore, these studies have shown that highly trained and highly skilled workforces are more likely to have advanced technical equipment because they have the competence to select the most useful advanced technology; that they are also more able to avoid long term machine breakdowns; and that they have the know-how to use modern computer-based production planning methods. Incredibly, the evidence therefore indicates, that advanced technology and high quality workforces are not a matter about which there can be an either–or choice; companies which wish to have one must have the other too. The implication is that the high-technology future, which is already present in many countries, requires the development of highly qualified and highly skilled workforces.

Many of these findings emerged in a study carried out by Daly, Hitchens and Wagner, who visited 32 manufacturing firms in West Germany and Britain during 1983–4. The aim of their study was to investigate the factors which might be important in explaining the much higher productivity of West Germany's manufacturing industry. As Daly et al. commented, 'by the mid-1970s German output per employee in manufacturing as a whole was about 50 per cent higher than in Britain, and higher still in mechanical engineering and vehicle production' (Daly et al., 1985, p.48). These productivity differentials had apparently remained more or less unchanged into the 1980s.

From previous research, they knew that the difference in productivity could not be simply related to the age of the machinery used in German and British industry: machinery in Britain was not obviously out of date. It was possible, however, that German machinery was more specialised and this might account for productivity differences.

They were also conscious of the difference in skill levels of West German and British workers. They asked:'Can it be that British productivity would be significantly improved if the typical worker were a trained and qualified person as in Germany?' (ibid., p.49). They noted that whereas two-thirds of German workers had passed qualifying examinations at a level equivalent to the British City and Guilds part II examinations, under a third of the British workforce had. Their own evidence from the metal-working trades of West Germany and Britain confirmed massive productivity differentials. They took six British firms and six West German firms which were a close match and compared actual outputs of machines per unit of time. They found the German firms to have a higher productivity than their British counterparts, ranging from 10 to 130 per cent higher.

On examining the machinery being used, skill differences and raw materials, they concluded that the most important factor was skills.

> Perhaps the most important overall implication of this study is that lack of technical expertise and training, rather than a simple lack of modern machinery is the stumbling block. (Ibid., p.59)

It is worth referring to their findings on machinery in order to underline their conclusion. In a number of respects they found no appreciable differences between West Germany and Britain. Thus, manning levels measured in terms of direct workers, machine running speeds, and the age of the machinery were much the same in both countries.

Where there were differences related to machinery, these could sometimes be seen to have their basis in differences in technical expertise and skill. The German firms had more advanced machinery (for example, more numerically controlled machines) and less serious problems with machine breakdowns than the British ones. The more advanced technology in the German firms seemed to be linked to the presence of more technical skill among decision makers. 'British plants often seemed not to appreciate the full potential of the new technology' (ibid., p.54). Firms in both countries experienced problems in relation to newly introduced machinery, but in Germany these were 'teething problems', whereas in Britain firms had experienced more breakdowns and continuous or long-standing problems. This was linked to the low level of skill in the British production and maintenance workforces.

Other differences in respect of machinery were found in the greater use in West Germany of mechanised feeding of materials (which cut down the numbers of indirect workers) and the fact that British firms purchased overseas machinery whereas German firms bought German machinery.

But, as we have already observed, Daly et al. emphasised the importance of differences of expertise and skill. These differences were evident at all levels of the firms. The German shop floor workers were twice as likely as the British ones to have an apprenticeship type qualification (half as against a quarter). Even more striking were the differences at management level. It is worth quoting in full their remarks about the differences at the foreman level:

> In fourteen of the sixteen British firms we visited the production foremen (as distinct from maintenance foremen) had acquired their position purely as a result of experience on the shop-floor, without formal qualifications. In contrast, German production foremen in all sixteen firms had passed examinations as craftsmen, thirteen had also acquired the higher certificate of *Meister* (master craftsman), and the remaining three had undergone additional training towards that qualification but had not yet passed their tests. (Ibid., p.56)

Above the level of foreman, amongst senior staff, yet further contrasts were found. All of those they met in the German factories were qualified engineers, save one who was a qualified technician. In Britain most of the firms' senior positions were filled by people with a sales or financial background or people who had learnt on the job.

The different compositions of the senior staff seemed to be a very important factor in explaining the difference in the machinery purchased – British firms buying less advanced equipment.

This may also have been the basis for the very different management organisations found in the West German and British firms respectively. It was observed that the latter included more specialist back-up roles – maintenance workers, production controllers, quality controllers – working parallel to the foremen. The people in specialist roles had formal technical training, whereas the production foremen had in the main little more than informal training on the job. Daly et al. suggest that necessity rather than preference dictated the British approach to management organisation: it was necessary because of the scarcity of trained persons.

We can sum up the implications of their research by saying that more investment in training was needed to tackle the lack of technical expertise at the top of firms, the lack of technical competence amongst foremen, and the shortage of craft training and training for the unskilled.

But their research also suggested that many of the senior British managers were technically ignorant, and we may wonder whether they would value greater expenditure on training for technical expertise and skill. After all, it was these same managers who had been responsible for buying machinery which was technically unsophisticated.

Furthermore, their research also found evidence of attitudes which were short sighted and pessimistic, and thus, unlikely to favour the investment in people's skills which may pay off in the long term. What the researchers describe as complacency and even despondency might also be termed the fatalism of British management:

> Too often amongst British firms we found an air of complacency, and even of despondency; one director suggested his business was unlikely to last more than fifteen years 'by which time I will have retired'. At another firm – an old-established family firm – the owner seemed unaware of the existence of appropriate new technology (computer numerically controlled machine tools). 'We are not interested in productivity here', he said; faster and more up-to-date machines 'present no special advantage and there is usually more to go wrong'. Moreover, he noted, 'the faster the machines work, the sooner the job is completed and the more setting that will be required'. While not wishing to over-generalise from such remarks, it

has to be said that we did not come across similar views in Germany. (Ibid., p.52)

The findings of a similar study of the furniture industry in West Germany and Britain provided an even worse picture of the poor state of training in Britain (Steedman and Wagner, 1987). For this study, the researchers visited eight West German and nine British firms engaged in the manufacture of fitted kitchens during 1986–7. They found a massive productivity advantage in favour of the West German plants, which appeared to reflect a vastly more advanced technological set up and an incomparably better qualified workforce.

The West German factories were making high quality fitted kitchens in small batches using computer numerically controlled (CNC) machinery. Moreover, the factories used much less indirect labour because the machinery was linked together so that feeding and offloading work was eliminated. The British factories were using up to date but technically inferior machinery to turn out lower quality products in large batches. The researchers were much impressed by the superior production planning in West German factories and the absence of proper planning in the British ones.

The difference in qualifications was even more startling than in the earlier study of the metal-working trades. Nearly everyone in the German factories was qualified, whereas practically nobody in the British firms was:

in Germany... in all the furniture-making companies visited at least 90 per cent of employees working on shop floor production had undergone a three-year [day-release] training course and obtained an examined vocational qualification comparable to our City and Guilds craft level...

In some British firms it was thought that no employees held the corresponding City and Guild certificates; in others, a few older employees were time-served craftsmen but had passed no examinations; in none of the British firms did the proportion time-served or holding a recognised vocational qualification exceed 10 per cent of shop floor employees.... About half of all German employees who had obtained a vocational qualification had done so as a woodworking machinist. (Steedman and Wagner, 1987, pp.91–2)

The situation looked worse the more it was examined in detail. It was not just the matter of the proportions qualified. It was also a matter of just how thorough and exhaustive the assessment of competence was in Germany, the higher ratio of new trainees, and the seriousness of the training effort in the West German factories.

The German apprentices had to take written examinations in topics such as the technology of their industry, language, and mathematics; and they had to take practical trade tests lasting 12 hours over two days. The British apprentices were not in the main required to take City and Guilds examinations at craft level: they were merely required to 'serve their time'.

In the West German factories there was one technical apprentice for every 20 employees – in Britain there was one craft apprentice or trainee for every hundred employees.

In West Germany the larger firms had set up trainee workshops and the smaller ones only allowed trainees onto the main production line in their third year. In Britain the trainees were put to work on the shop floor from the start of their apprenticeship. The wisdom of putting apprentices straight onto the shop floor in the British factories might be dubious from a training point of view – but it might also be challenged from a safety point of view: 'a shop floor laden with complex, heavy and dangerous machinery is not wholly a suitable training environment' (ibid., p.92).

The picture regarding the training of foremen resembled that found in the earlier study of metal-working. The German foremen had their basic craft qualifications and some had trained beyond that. The foremen in charge of maintenance, for example, held a *Meister* qualification. The British foremen, in contrast, did not normally hold any formal qualifications but had been promoted to foremen on the basis of their experience of the shop floor.

Retraining for CNC technology was taken very seriously in West Germany and could last between a couple of weeks and six months. 'In Britain, "a few days" retaining was often regarded as adequate to equip an operator for new CNC machinery' (ibid., p.93).

In the light of all these unflattering comparisons, some consternation about the state of British training seems well justified. Steedman and Wagner pulled no punches with their judgement:

> The net effect of these technological and organisational differences was that the typical German and typical British firms that we visited were visibly of different calibre. Both had access on international markets to the same selection of modern machinery, but the qualifications of those employed were entirely different. (Ibid., p.94)

They seem to be saying here that the technology problem was less important than the people problem: you can buy new machinery easily, but developing a skilled and competent workforce takes longer. What they do not directly deal with is the question of why management has neglected the development of the workforce. Having said that, it is possible to read between the lines of other remarks made by them that the source of the problem is to be found in management attitudes.

For example, they found that German and British managers had radically different views on investment. German firms regarded investment in new CNC and CAD/CAM systems as vital for competitive performance.

No British managers saw competitive pressures of this sort as the most important criterion of investment in new technology...British firms were indeed renewing their machinery stock quite frequently, but not upgrading the technology of the machinery they acquired to the same extent as German firms. (Ibid., p.89)

This no doubt reflected the poor levels of technical expertise and training in management; as Steedman and Wagner put it, the British managers seemed less aware of the possibilities. 'Machinery in Britain is often as new as in Germany...but it is not as technically advanced; there seemed often to be a lack of appreciation of the full production possibilities that have become available with modern technology' (ibid., p.94). But it also seemed to reflect a lack of enterprising spirit amongst British managers. This may be read into the comment made by the researchers on the view of the managers with respect to their current situation:

Many British kitchen firms are undoubtedly successful in the products that they make – and with the lower productivity and lower wages that go with them. They say (as it was put to us): 'we just concentrate on what we're good at'. (Ibid., p.94)

Enterprising managers would be seeking the productivity rises and improved quality which new technology and a highly skilled workforce would produce. They would seek them because that is the way to hold off the increasing competitive pressures from Europe and from the rest of the world (global competition as the White Paper *Employment for the 1990s* called it). That is the way to develop a sound business for the increasingly knowledge based production of the future.

A third study, this time of the women's outerwear manufacturers in Britain and West Germany produced very similar results (Steedman and Wagner, 1989). The researchers found that German factories had achieved higher productivity than their British counterparts making clothing of a comparable quality: 'Germany produced roughly twice as many garments per employee as Britain' (ibid., p.42). This time the machinery was more modern in the factories of West Germany, but again there were the familiar differences in machine breakdowns, production planning and skills. And again the researchers emphasised the importance of the high standards of training for the success of the West German firms, which were concentrating on small batches of high quality garments. The British firms were, by contrast, engaged in the manufacture of cheaper, standardised clothes made in larger batches.

And again it was not just the production workers who were better qualified. There was a major difference in the qualifications of the managements in the two countries:

> In all the German plants visited, the owner or plant manager had completed a three-year clothing apprenticeship; in addition, over two-thirds had followed a two or three year full-time course in clothing technology (at a level corresponding to our HND/BSc). It was exceptional to find British managers with a similar level of specialist training; most had no technical qualifications specifically relating to the clothing industry. (Ibid., pp.50–1)

THE PROBLEM FOR AND WITH MANAGEMENT

Employers sometimes blame each other for the lack of training in Britain. This really relates to the training of employees in general skills which are in general demand in labour markets. Some employers are not prepared to train their own staff through apprenticeships and rely on picking up all the skilled workers they need through the labour market. Obviously this is only possible if some employers continue to offer apprenticeships. These skilled workers can then be 'poached'.

It is very difficult to imagine a time when employers would cease to poach if the extra cost of inducing skilled labour to leave the firms that trained them always remained below the cost to the employer of carrying out the training. Appeals to operate against this simplistic calculation of economic self-interest are unlikely to work in a system in which laissez-faire sentiments are endowed with moral and even religious value.

Poaching is a logical and rational course of action, within any system of competitive market forces, in the allocation and distribution of labour. Since such competition distributes labour in Germany and Britain, the latter should not have any worse record on training in general skills than West Germany. But it has. The explanation for this difference is due partly to the role of public regulation, which we will consider shortly; and partly to management's organisation, culture, and, currently, its mood.

The nature of management organisation in Britain is such that managers with a background and 'feel' for production issues are thinly represented in top management, which is made up of sales and finance people – even in manufacturing. This leads to a devaluing of the task of organising production (by which we mean the 'making' of goods or services). Consequently the necessity to properly fund production activities is often lacking as a balance sheet mentality cuts and trims items which are essential for long term productivity gains but are simply 'costs' in cost accounting methods. Lacking a direct under-standing of the processes which have to be developed, improved and reorganised to search out greater productivity, higher quality, and more flexibility – all esssential in the contemporary world of international competition – they fail to invest in the only type of workforce that can deliver the modern technology. This is a high quality workforce, well trained from the production floor, through the strata of intermediate management and up to the top level of management.

The management culture in Britain still smacks of what was a long time ago the self-evident ideal of the gentleman-amateur (Laski, 1940). This ideal, presented in its stereotypical form, was essentially that the English gentleman should maintain towards life 'an attitude of indifferent receptivity', being 'interested in nothing in a professional way', and having hobbies rather than a vocation (ibid., p.13). When it came to education, the English gentleman knew 'that much learning is ungainly, and in any case drives men mad' (ibid., p.18). His practical (amateurish) approach had its own anti-sccence and anti-technology impact on industry – both were paid inadequate attention and down-played.

Amateurism today is as evident at the level of junior management and supervisor as anywhere. Managers at this level are selected for their general managerial skills, because top management see management exclusively as an abstract process, that is, a process of coordination and gaining cooperation. Technical requirements relating to the concrete nature of production activities are ignored or underestimated. Cynically it might be wondered whether the gifted amateurs at higher levels feel safer promoting other gifted amateurs who operate as they do.

On the other hand, there is little choice, or so it seems, to promoting people on the basis of on the job experience. It was only in the late 1980s that concern over the state of management education galvanised a certain amount of activity by industry and commerce on the construction of a more substantial system of management education, training and development.

Finally, management in some sectors, but certainly not all, is demoralised and fatalistic. This is very apparent in the small manufacturing sector. Lacking a vision of how to manage the transition to the high-tech future, the issue of human resource management is merely a trendy fad covered in the specialist management literature. Why train? What's the use? It's just a matter of time anyway.

TRADE UNION ACTION ON TRAINING

The old apprenticeship system was created and maintained by the efforts of 'tradesmen' (and since they were nearly totally male we shall use that gender to describe them), skilled workers who were committed to preserving social standards and a certain way of life as well as technical skills.

To have become a tradesman was to have acquired a *concern* for the quality of the work, as well as having acquired the technical skills to produce good quality work.

This concern was drilled into the apprentice by the trained craftsman on the job. The apprentices were assigned to time-served men who would act as role models. The apprentices would watch and imitate the skilled men, and the latter would watch the apprentices' work, ensuring that they did it properly.

But of course there was more to it than that. Each day the time-served men would have a multitude of opportunities to teach the apprentice a *morality* of working. This morality touched on 'doing the job properly', 'getting the job done and not taking liberties' and 'being well respected'.

The trade unionists were not only involved in instruction of apprentices in work skills (and social ideas), they also played, at times, a crucial role in the testing and certification processes. One old tradesmen, a carpenter, described to us in the late 1970s his experience of getting a union card some forty years earlier.

When anyone went for a union ticket – I'm going chippy-wise – I should imagine it was the same for plumbers, painters and what have you – but chippy wise – anyone who went for a ticket, they used to have to go up to the branch they fancied, get someone to propose them and second them at the branch. Then you go before the branch and there is all the people round. They would be asking you specific questions pertaining to your trade – questions they knew you should know. How would you go about fitting up a staircase? How would you do a newel post? How would you start constructing a door? You would get all these questions and when they finished questioning you – and then they have some bloody awkward questions – when they finished questioning you, 'Would you mind waiting outside Mr White?' You go outside, or down in the bar in my case. I was having a pint when, '*Brother* White, will you come in?' Now I know I've been made a member. But they were discussing it for ten minutes between themselves: whether I was capable for having a ticket. So you had to fight to get in a union (Interview notes).

There were a lot of non-union firms paying less than the union rate for the job. But they had a reputation for 'bodging'. People who wanted jobs done properly went to firms that employed trade union labour. With certain trades, a union ticket was an automatic advert to the quality of the worker.

By the 1980s, the craft apprenticeship system in Britain had broken down. The decline had been deepening for decades. Even by the inter-war period it had already declined so much in engineering that 'the majority of youths entering the industry did not serve their time' (Jefferys, 1946, p.205). The numbers coming through the apprentice-ship system fell sharply in the late 1970s and early 1980s. For example, the numbers starting the Engineering Industrial Training Board's recommended off-the-job training for craft and technician apprentice-ships fell from 24 000 in 1974–5 to 23 000 in 1979–80, then down to 11 000 in 1982–2 (Pearson, Hutt and Parsons, 1984, p.140).

With the passing of craft trade unionism and craft apprenticeships, the British trade union movement has not ceased to be vitally concerned with education and training. In the late 1980s the TUC drew attention to the situation in Britain. The 1989 Congress debated the issue of training and accepted the view that the workforce was undereducated, undertrained, underskilled and underpaid. Politically, the union movement found itself in great difficulties because it wished to participate in national policymaking on training but the attitude and ideology of the Thatcher Government made such participation impossible.

PUBLIC AUTHORITY

More than twenty years ago, Williams (1963) examined practices in seven West European countries and found that the state in those countries had actively organised industrial training.

The state in Britain, in contrast, concerned itself with training belatedly and reluctantly. At first it was mainly involved in the superintendance of training through the Industrial Training Act 1964. This Act created industrial training boards which were made responsible for the amount and quality of training carried out. These bodies each covered a particular industry, provided grants to firms undertaking training and raised money for training from a levy on employers.

Throughout the 1970s and 1980s the British state spent increasingly large amounts on training and provided substantial training directly. In the 1980s commentators often accused the Thatcher Government of expanding youth training to bring down unemployment figures rather than to equip the nation with a highly skilled workforce.

THE TRAINING CRISIS

Britain, we have seen, has relatively few qualified people in key sectors and key jobs. It has a chronic history of skill shortages acting as bottlenecks on industrial expansion. And because of low skills and poor vocational training it is losing out in the international competition between advanced capitalist economies to achieve the production of high quality products at high levels of productivity using the most advanced technology available.

We have also seen that the British state hung back, unlike its other European counterparts, from actively organising industrial training.

The state did become more heavily involved in the organisation of training – mainly through the use of public funds for training in the 1980s – but the problems of low skill persist.

Employers are trapped in a culture which places little value on training and they need help to change. That change has got to be organised. By the end of the 1980s it was obvious to even the most die-hard laissez-faire adherent that the state must become involved in confronting the training crisis. The White Paper *Employment for the 1990s* was the Thatcher Government's recognition of the need for the state to do something. Further recognition came in January 1990 when the newly appointed Employment Secretary, Michael Howard, said he planned to make improved training his main priority (*The Guardian*, 5 January 1990).

But, as has become evident from the experience of Britain in the 1980s, the state's involvement has got to be a sophisticated one, and one that does not reproduce low skill. Incredible as it may seem, it is possible, as the Youth Training Scheme (YTS) demonstrates and which we outline in Chapter 4, for the state to intervene in training, apparently showing that it believes training to be important, whilst at the same time intervening in a way that fails to deliver the essence of real training – skill. Further, the evidence from Britain's YTS experience shows that the state has even ended up 'counterfeiting' skilled labour. What we mean by this is explored below, but the price to be paid for this failure of state intervention in vocational training is confusion as well as lack of real movement towards economic viability. State intervention into training has to be competent and skilled if the task of raising skill levels in the British workforce is to be really achieved.

3 Equality at Work

INTRODUCTION

Discrimination in the labour market is a longstanding problem. It exists because employers make recruitment, training and promotion decisions on grounds which are irrelevant from the point of view of the economic performance of the labour concerned. Their decisions should be based on characteristics such as price and productiveness, but instead they are guided by ones to which they should be indifferent such as gender, race, age, and able-bodiedness. The specific labour involved – the people subject to discrimination – is devalued. Under the pure model of market forces, this devaluation should not exist, in reality it does, and has existed for a very long time.

The pure economic forces of the market should lead to this undervalued labour being recruited by employers who can bring down their costs by employing it; and the consequent rise in demand for the undervalued labour should bring its price and real worth back into line. But the fact that discrimination persists shows that there are contingent circumstances which prevent the market from working in this way.

The victims of discrimination end up rejected by the labour market, unemployed, underemployed, or confined to low paying and poor jobs. From the point of view of society it represents a massive waste, with skills and talent being squandered. It is not an exaggeration to say that the scale and duration of employment discrimination in Britain make it one of the most severe of the crises which trouble the labour market.

It is this dynamic that we want to uncover in this chapter. There is a considerable amount of evidence to demonstrate that the labour market is riven with discrimination against a considerable number of people who have different characteristics. This discrimination is reproduced through certain activities within that labour market even though there may not be a direct economic reason for the market recreating such discrimination. We will demonstrate that the genesis of that discrimination is to be found in social relations that are external to the market. This underlines the way in which we have approached the whole question of labour throughout the book. The causes for labour market activity cannot be understood purely by looking at the market itself – they need a wider understanding of social relations.

TIGHTENING MARKETS AND DISCRIMINATION

Whilst the major part of this chapter will detail the way in which discrimination outside the labour market is reproduced within it, there are clear strands within the internal relationship between capital and labour at work which, under certain circumstances, take part in recreating such discrimination. The international conditions within which British monopoly capital has grown have been dependent upon imperialism. The resultant racism has imbued nearly all social relationships within British society and between British society and others. The capital that was creating labour market conditions with British workers was firmly linked to the capital that was creating different labour markets in the Indian subcontinent, in Africa and the Carribean. Since capital will attempt to purchase labour as cheaply as it can, it will construct different sets of social relations in different countries, if it is allowed to, in order to obtain that labour as cheaply as possible. The particular relationship in which British capital was engaged in creating these condition also created a set of international relationships, within which racism flourished.

However, in the tightening labour market that will exist in Britain in the 1990s, it will be in the interests of sections of British capital to be able to draw its labour from as large a pool as possible. This should involve the whole of society and should lead to a realisation that, for these sections of capital, racism and sexism are counterproductive. However, as we shall see, it is no simple matter to simply drop an ideology when it is inconvenient.

The Thatcher Government's White Paper, called *Employment for the 1990s*, drew attention to the demographic trends and urged employers to place more emphasis on training and to look to new sources of labour.

> Employers will have to retrain their existing staff to adapt to changes rather than rely on the market for ready-trained young people. In addition, employers cannot expect to recruit as many young people, especially well-qualified young people, as they have in the past. (Employment Department, 1988, p.7)

Employers were told that they would have to turn to substitutes for young workers – it was said they would need women, ethnic minorities, and older workers. These alternative sources of labour are *possible* substitutes for young workers; and the possibilities have been made the basis of predictions (there will be more women in the labour force), the basis of proposals (we need to change attitudes on the use of older workers who want to work beyond retirement age) and the basis of new aspirations (the employment of people with disabilities should now be increased).

But the temporary state of the labour market offers no permanent solution to discrimination. Firstly, labour markets are themselves very affected by developments in the population, which, as the British post war experience shows, do not just depend on birth rates. In the 1950s when health services, transport and other low-paid industries were short of labour, British population was rapidly supplemented by migrant workers from Commonwealth countries. In other words, the make-up of a population is subject to processes of emigration and immigration. The demographic projections for the 1990s, for example, may be substantially overturned as a result of population movements unleashed by the completion in Europe of the single market in labour, which is part of the package of reforms of the Single European Act agreed in 1987 and intended to bring about a single 'common' market in the European Community by 1992.

Secondly, decades, and in some cases centuries, of discrimination are not wiped out by a temporary tightening of labour market conditions due to demographic trends. The possibility of employers turning to women, ethnic minorities, older people and people with disabilities may be partially or totally blocked both by the discrimination of employers and by the way in which it is recreated in the rest of society. It will be some years before we can be sure just what is going to happen in this respect, but the early evidence is not promising. A 1989 postal survey of nearly 2000 employers, commissioned by the Training Agency and the National Economic Development Office (NEDO), confirmed that many employers had experienced difficulties in recruiting young people and were expecting difficulties in the future. The majority of employers surveyed were not, however, turning to other sources of labour. They were instead, intensifying their efforts to recruit young people (*Labour Market Quarterly Report*, November 1989, p.16). Employers have not simply learnt the demographic message, their discriminatory ideology seems to triumph on occasions over their economic self interest in a tightening labour market.

WOMEN AND DISCRIMINATION

Sex discrimination is not just due to the subjective state of mind of employers – it is not some arbitrary, free-standing quirk of their mental outlook. It has played a significant role in structuring the social and economic relations of labour throughout history.

Within the pre-industrial world this took a variety of forms, but in that era, within the working population the role of the family contained a fusion of roles that have since become separated. Under the process of industrialisation, the state and civil society have replaced some of those earlier roles. The state is involved in organising and providing education and training, it has made arrangements for welfare and social security, and a large part of society's production of goods and services takes place within privately owned businesses and public sector organisations.

Much work still occurs within the family home – mostly unpaid work of caring, socialising children, cooking and cleaning. Some estimates suggest that the amount of time spent in this type of work exceeds that spent in paid labour. Domestic labour and its relation to paid labour is the subject of complex debates (Gardiner, 1976; Hurstfield, 1978; Beechey and Perkins, 1987).

The changing form of labour, from work carried out within the family sphere to that carried out as wage labour, has been the backdrop to a struggle between the sexes over the gender division of labour in society. Feminist writers argue that industrialisation, with the accompanying separation of the family and the economic spheres, was attended by much conflict and a struggle to define culturally a sexual division of labour. Leonore Davidoff (1979) makes precisely this point when she says that 'in the period 1780 to 1850, the definition of masculinity and femininity, together with their social location in work and home, became an arena of conflict' (Davidoff, 1979, p.64). The continuing struggle between the sexes over entry into the world of paid employment during this century has been documented in detail by Walby (1986).

The sexual division of labour is not 'natural'. It is a social construction which is made and remade.

The existence of the different categories of domestic and paid labour is often ignored *because* it is taken as natural that women will do domestic work for the family and will only break into paid employment as and when that is compatible with the integrity of the family.

The main barrier to women's involvement and participation in paid employment is the current social system surrounding the family. The involvement and participation of women in paid employment depends also on the contours of the sexual division of labour in both the paid employment sector and in the family or homework sector. In other words, if women are to enter more into paid employment, they have to be freed from responsibility for domestic work. This may be accomplished both by men taking on a larger share of domestic, unpaid labour, and by more of the family's needs for child care and domestic labour being met by labour activity which is paid. It is this aspect of the relationship between paid labour and social relationships entirely external to the labour market that presents one of the clearest examples of our general thesis.

At the very end of the 1980s this was discussed most clearly within the concept developed by Peter Moss of the work-family relationship (Moss, 1989). This concept deals with the issue of child care and its relationship to the labour market as not only a labour force issue but also a women's issue, a men's issue and a children's issue. Policy on child care has failed to deal with it in this rounded way and, until it does, married women with dependent children will experience difficulties in entering the labour force to their and the economy's fullest potential.

CURRENT PROBLEMS OF DISCRIMINATION AGAINST WOMEN

The proportion of women working *only* in the family home is continuing to decrease and the proportion in the UK paid workforce has been rising: in 1960, 35 per cent of all UK employees were women, in 1970 it was 38 per cent, but by 1986 it was up to 45 per cent (*Employment Gazette*, Historical Supplement No 2, October 1987).

But, and this a very large but, the women are not only becoming an increasing part of the national paid workforce, they are also continuing to do nearly all the domestic work. There is, in fact, evidence from the *British Social Attitudes Survey 1984* that in most marriages it was women that mainly did the washing and ironing, preparation of the evening meal, household cleaning, household shopping, and, importantly, looking after children when they are sick. The only household task which was done mainly by men was repairing household equipment (Halsey, 1987, p.14).

In practice many women have not moved into paid labour on a full time basis – they have taken part-time jobs (Beechey and Perkins, 1987). In 1985 the vast majority (78 per cent) of men in employment were full-time permanent employees, only half (49 per cent) of women were. In this respect, the gap in the labour market status of men and women was greater in the UK than in many other countries of the European Community.

Furthermore, according to the 1988 Labour Force Survey, the high rate of part-time working amongst women is mainly concentrated amongst married women. Whereas non-married women employees were predominantly in full-time jobs, a majority of married women employees were in part-time jobs (*Employment Gazette*, April 1989, p.184).

Married women go into part-time paid work rather than full-time paid work because they have to carry on doing the caring, cooking, and cleaning for themselves as well as the rest of the family. Whilst they are encouraged to enter paid employment, there is very little help or support for women who are in paid employment – for example, Britain's childcare services are notoriously deficient by European standards (Moss, 1989). Without such help and support the women find the attempt to reconcile domestic labour for the family and paid labour crucifyingly difficult.

In the 1980s, after the recession at the beginning of the decade, many of the new jobs created in Britain were filled by women workers. The jobs were often part-time ones and the women were often married. Indeed, 72 per cent of the net increase in employees in employment in the five years from 1984 to 1988 were accounted for by married women! (See *Employment Gazette*, April 1989, Table 4, p.185.) Evidence from changes in the unemployment rate and the economic activity rate suggest that many of these were women being drawn into the labour market from full time domestic labour rather than from the category of official unemployment.

This may seem to contradict the idea that there are barriers to women entering paid labour due to the family and the nature of domestic labour. But it would be very unwise to take the trend between 1984 and 1988 and simply project it into the future. Women who entered paid employment in those years may have been able to cope with both domestic labour and part-time paid employment, but this does not mean the rest were in a position to do so – given the existing employment packages and childcare facilities available.

Moreover, if more and more of the new employment opportunities were simply jobs that young people were no longer filling, there would be other problems as well. One pessimistic view of the ability of women to move into the labour market was evident in a 1989 report from the Employment Institute (Employment Institute, May 1989). It suggested that women were not likely to be attracted back to do the work traditionally performed by minimum-age school leavers. Given that the costs of returning to work have been borne by the prospective returnees, rather than by the state or employers, it is often impossible to make enough money in low paid jobs to re-enter the labour market.

The difficulties for women of carrying out both domestic labour for the family and paid work also appears in other ways. Women have to try to fit their paid work into a life already full of caring and working for the family. They are often caught between inflexible employers who will not change their hours of work and inflexible partners who will not change their hours of leisure. After a while they come to feel that the low rewards, the regimented work and the difficulties of managing childcare are just not worth it. The result is that many women start low-paid part-time jobs in retail, hotels and other service sector jobs and leave within a short time. For example, the turnover rates in retail are astronomical. Jarvis and Prais recently reported that 'perhaps half of employees of all ages leave within a year' whilst in large cities 'with plentiful employment opportunities, labour turnover rates of "100 or 200 per cent a year" were frequently mentioned' (Jarvis and Prais, 1989, p.58).

Another sign of the conflict between domestic labour and paid labour experienced by married women is the higher absenteeism rates of women with children. Employers sometimes explain a preference for hiring men on the basis that they have less time off than women. There are official statistics which confirm that women do have more absences from work, but this evidence also indicates that men and women without dependent children have the same absence rates, and that men with dependent children have more time off because of their own illness or injury than do women with dependent children (see the General Household Survey of 1984). The implication seems clear – women in total have a higher rate of absence because those with dependent children take time off to look after them when they are ill.

In this section of the present chapter we have explored the relationship between women's experiences in the labour market and their experiences in the family. We conclude that, whilst the possibility of entering the labour market is formally open to all women, and is promised to them on equal terms to men by the legislation of the 1970s, it is subjected to limits imposed by the civil society which surrounds that market, especially the social relations of family life. But the trend in the economic life of Britain towards greater participation by married women in paid work is threatening the gender division of labour. Given the strength of the discrimination faced by women, however, the experience of women is full of consequent contradictions – not least the necessity of doing both domestic work and paid work in a situation where they lack the necessary rights, means and resources to do both.

LABOUR MARKET SEGMENTATION

Discrimination in the labour market has produced a division of labour which is marked by occupational and industrial segregation of female labour (Rubery and Tarling, 1988, p.112). Thus it is women who are mainly employed in health, welfare and education professions, in clerical jobs, as secretaries and shop assistants, and in personal service occupations. In contrast, men manage and administrate; they are engineers and scientists, technicians and craftsmen; and they are in the armed forces.

This pattern has resulted from historical forces which have shaped and moulded the structure of paid employment. Attempts to understand these forces have at times made use of the dual labour market theory with its notions of 'primary' and 'secondary' sectors. Primary sector jobs are relatively secure and well paid, have good working conditions and chances of advancement; whereas the secondary sector jobs are insecure, marginal, badly paid, have poor working conditions, little training and little chance of advancement, and are subject to harsh and arbitrary management. The primary sector jobs are filled by white males and the secondary sector ones by women, ethnic minorities and other disadvantaged groups.

According to Michael Piore, one of the writers who developed this theory, the key factors in the process of structuring jobs in the two sectors are employer and trade union policies and actions (Piore, 1975, pp.353–4). He says the unions, which were based in the primary sector, pursued employment security and employers responded by creating employment stabilisation in the primary and unionised sector and by exporting job insecurity to the secondary non-unionised sector.

This theory, especially as stated baldly here, leaves a lot unanswered. Why for example was the labour market bifurcated in the first place? Why was there, in other words, a secondary sector to which insecurity could be exported? Where is the evidence that the labour market is structured into just two distinct sectors? And if there are not just two sectors, how many sectors are there?

It is not difficult to supply some manner of answers to these questions, but, in our view, the model remains seriously inadequate for reasons identified by feminist writers. Firstly, it contains insufficient analysis of the processes through which men obtain and maintain control over primary sector jobs (Beechey and Perkins, 1987, p.137). Secondly, it is deficient in its treatment of supply side factors, and here again it is a matter of paying attention to factors outside the labour market in order to understand what goes on within it. In particular, it has been seen as necessary, in revising the dual labour market theory, to conceptualise the structuring of the labour market as being partly determined by the system of social reproduction (ibid., 1987, p.138).

More recent work stresses the need to look outside the labour market for the explanation of segmentation, that is, it is not employer policies nor union policies alone which create labour market segmentation, but also the social system and its organisation of social reproduction.

WOMEN, EDUCATION AND TRAINING

Education and training are part of the supply side processes which construct the labour market, and are in turn constructed by that market. They are also part of the processes through which labour power is reproduced. Consequently they play an important role in the way in which inequalities between women and men are produced and reproduced.

At school girls and boys learn that they are to follow different destinies: the girls take 'girls' subjects' and the boys take 'boys' subjects'. This split between the sexes is then officially confirmed and certified; the girls do better in 'O' level/CSE exams in English, French, arts, commercial and domestic subjects, while the boys succeed better in mathematics, sciences and technology. The schooling process is rounded off under the subtle pressures of parental attitudes – with girls being sent the message that it is not as important for them as for boys to stay on at school.

Whilst more young women than young men undertake full-time study at 'A' level, it is women and not men who are under-represented in higher education: in 1985–6 women students formed only two-fifths of all those in higher education (*Labour Market Quarterly Report*, July 1988, p.15). And it used to be even worse than this. Of course the vast majority of young people do not go into higher education, but amongst the educationally privileged there are important gender differences. Whilst the men are more likely go on to higher education in order to take degrees, women are more likely to leave school and take vocational courses or professional courses.

Access to YTS in the 1980s showed how gender segregation is carried through into training, even though the provision was supposed to be based on formal equality of training opportunity. Not only were women under-represented in YTS as a whole (43 per cent of people starting YTS in 1987–8 were women), but they were also concentrated in female areas of work. Thus, according to Training Agency data, three-quarters of young women who started in 1987–8 were located in clerical, sales and personal services (*Labour Market Quarterly Report*, October 1988, p.16).

What is the result of the different education and training experiences of women and men? Women employees are less likely to be qualified, and are less likely to be well qualified, than male employees (*Labour Market Quarterly Report*, May 1989, p.20). In consequence, women enter the labour market on a different basis to men, and enjoy employment and advancement prospects which are distinctly inferior to those of men.

DISCRIMINATION AGAINST ETHNIC MINORITIES

The discrimination against black people inside the labour market, as we have already said, is related to racism in social relationships outside the market. This racism was the historical product of international relations based on British monopoly capital and imperialism. Much of contemporary racism is directed against black ethnic minorities, but racism is not new in British society – for example, Irish and Jewish migrants in the 19th century were the focus of much racism.

The crisis in the labour market situation of the black ethnic minorities has persisted in one or other of its two major forms for nearly 40 years. From the 1950s onwards, black ethnic minorities have been, firstly, diverted into jobs with lower pay and status than their white counterparts with the same or equivalent skills and qualifications, and, secondly, they have been subject to much higher rates of unemployment. Both of these forms of inequality – in jobs and in unemployment – represents a labour market crisis, since as a process, the labour market should be ensuring that employers are able to obtain appropriately skilled and competent labour, whereas it has been functioning in a way which delivers white rather than black labour.

The state saw itself as trying to correct the malfunctioning of the labour market by means of legal regulation. First there was the Race Relations Act of 1968 and then there was the similarly named Act of 1976. These acts have not touched the problem of discrimination. It lives on. A recent British study found that at least 30 per cent of employers discriminated against Asian and West Indian job applicants (*Employment Report*, Vol VII, No.3, November 1986, p.4). In 1985, unemployment amongst people of working age was only 10.9 per cent amongst whites, but 20.7 per cent amongst ethnic minorities (*Employment Gazette*, April 1989, p.194).

These are not isolated research findings. Labour market research over twenty years, notably by PEP (Political and Economic Planning) and PSI (Policy Studies Institute), has demonstrated persistent discrimination against black workers with respect to unemployment, recruitment, job segregation, and promotion. Brown and Gay made the comment in their study that 'there has been no reduction in the extent of discrimination over the last decade' (Brown and Gay, 1985, p.33).

Racial discrimination not only occurs in British society, it is also *known* to occur. Brown reported very large proportions of white, West Indian and Asian women and men believing that recruitment and promotion decisions were made in some firms or organisations on the basis of race or colour (Brown, 1984, p.219, Table 117). Some twenty years after the first legislation aimed at abolishing discrimination in employment, the Thatcher Government, in *Employment for the 1990s*, was moved to say, in late 1988, that:

> Discrimination against ethnic minorities by employers is not only unlawful but it is also against their own commercial interests to cut themselves off from a source of skilled or potentially skilled labour. (Employment Department, 1988, pp.8–9)

The Government was, it seems, concerned about discrimination, and it chose to emphasise practical considerations for ending discrimination by employers. Why not more stress on the rights of black citizens? Perhaps it reflects the White Paper's focus on business health rather than on the rights of black citizens; or perhaps it was just the Government's judgement of which arguments would have more weight with British employers. Either way, the statement casts an interesting light on the thinking of the Thatcher Government at the end of the 1980s.

THE SOURCES OF RACISM

Ultimately the problem of race relations in Britain stems from the failure to resolve the racism and discrimination expressed in British social relations. After the Second World War migrant labour, mainly male workers, came to Britain from its former colonies, especially India, Pakistan, and the Caribbean. The neo-colonial experience, unemployment in their own countries and comparatively high wages in Britain led migrant workers to take jobs in the textile industry, public transport, the National Health Service and other low-paid sectors in the economy of the 'mother country'. The black migrant workers met with considerable hostility from the white population despite the alleged social bond formed by the common citizenship of the British Commonwealth.

This hostility, together with economic conditions, resulted in the racist laws on immigration which progressively tightened up entry into Britain in the 1960s, 70s and 80s. The continued potency of the 'mother country' ideology did mean, however, that the law made provision for the entry of the dependents of those who had come here to work. Without this ideology the law may have just permitted a controlled flow of temporary migrant workers as in West Germany. In the event, as Anwar has commented, 'It turned a movement of workers, many of whom were probably only interested in staying temporarily, into a relatively permanent immigration of families' (Anwar, 1986, p.9). Subsequent legislation and its racist application tightened up on the migration of dependents.

The immigration controls led to the long term restriction of black people entering Britain – but they did not actually confront the conflict between whites and black people. In fact they only made it worse. Indeed, since racism was a quality of that social relation, it could not therefore to be addressed by merely halting the numbers of black people coming to Britain. This racism could only be tackled by black people becoming a proper part of British society, that is, by creating a truly multi-racial and multi-cultural society.

Racism intensified *after* the 1962 Act as shown by the formation of the National Front in 1966, and this is further confirmed by the fact that some 16 years after that same Act, the leader of the Conservative Party, soon to be Prime Minister of Britain, Mrs Thatcher, stated that people were afraid that Britain and the British character might be swamped by people with a different culture (Anwar, 1986, p.87).

Whether or not Mrs Thatcher was a politician 'on the make', opportunistically seeking advantage from racism, is a matter of conjecture. A racist undertone, however, became a hall mark of the Conservative Party and was accompanied by a tough party policy on immigration controls in the 1980s.

The immigration controls, and the way they were operated, created a powerfully contradictory experience of the state for many people when placed alongside a public policy of equal opportunities. On one hand, white and black people could read off the view that black people were bearers of an alien culture which was threatening to swamp the British culture and this was so dangerous that black people had to be stopped from coming here. Simultaneously, people were told that the ethnic minority communities were making a valuable contribution to Britain and employers and others were exhorted to treat them equally and provide equal opportunities.

The falseness of this notion of good community relations was exposed by the quite different view taken by the Thatcher Government on the creation of a single European market by 1992. This single market was strongly supported by the Government even though it entailed the free movement of persons in the European Community. The Department of Trade and Industry explained what this meant for workers as follows:

> Nationals of Member States have the right to go to another Member State to look for work, or take up work, provided they comply with its laws or regulations on employment and have a valid passport or national identity card. They are then entitled to the same treatment as nationals of the 'host' Member State in matters of pay, working conditions, vocational training, income tax, social security and trade union rights. Their families may join them and enjoy the same rights. (Department of Trade and Industry, *The Single Market: The Facts* September 1988, p.67)

The persistence of institutionalsed racism also shows up in the alienation of ethnic minority communities from the democratic political process. Few people would challenge the *actuality* of this alienation, although some might argue that black ethnic minorities have a full *opportunity* to participate in the process. The most obvious evidence of their lack of involvement in the 1980s was the under-representation of ethnic minorities in the House of Commons and amongst local government councillors. Until four black MPs were elected in 1987, for the Labour Party, there had not been any black ethnic minority MPs in the House for many years. Even in London, where the Greater London Council, under Labour control, made serious efforts to involve ethnic minority communities in political life, the number of ethnic minority councillors was very low.

Less obviously, the democratic political process has been slow to involve black ethnic minority *communities* – as opposed to ethnic minority individuals. As a result of the experience of insecurity caused by the immigration controls and racial attacks and harrassment by racists, the migrants who established ethnic minority communities in the 1960s and 70s developed community organisations and institutions which could mobilise political support and intervene in the democratic process. By the 1970s and 80s many members of the black ethnic minority communities were most effectively involved in political life within their own community organisations and through their own community leaders.

Their exclusion from political life is important in the context of equal opportunity. Only by being fully involved will black ethnic minorities be able to ensure that the law and public services correspond to their needs as they see them. For example, equal employment opportunities can be influenced both by the laws on equality at work and by the educational and training systems provided by the state, and yet defects are to be found in all these areas from the point of view of equal opportunities.

ETHNIC MINORITIES AND UNEMPLOYMENT

The relationship between racial discrimination and unemployment is not a simple one; there is no one to one relationship between the level of discrimination and the degree of higher unemployment amongst ethnic minorities. Demonstrating this point is not easy, but some evidence of the complex link between discrimination and unemployment is provided by the different relationships to unemployment amongst different sections of ethnic minorities. Thus, West Indian women are thought to suffer relatively lower levels of unemployment than West Indian men. Although both suffer discrimination, it is claimed they react differently:

> West Indian men have been less conditioned to accept inferior wages, however, and have expectations of employment comparable to those

of their white working-class peers. In their case, higher rates of unemployment are the principal consequence of labour market disadvantage and discrimination. (Buck et al., 1986, p.176)

Different again, it has been claimed, is the Asian community in London who appear to experience lower levels of discrimination by avoiding the 'open' labour market. This is,

> because of the greater use made of ethnic networks in securing access to employment when the open market is inadequate; in this case 'crowding' is more appparent, with evidence of poor conditions and other forms of exploitation in work-places with predominantly Asian work-forces. (Ibid, p.176)

It is well known that the incidence of unemployment was disproportionately high amongst ethnic minority groups in the 1970s and 80s. With the fall in unemployment in the late 1980s, the gap between the whites' and ethnic minority groups' unemployment rates decreased. The rate amongst whites fell from 11.4 per cent in 1984 to 8.5 per cent in 1988, and amongst ethnic minority people it fell from 21.4 per cent to 13.5 per cent (*Employment Gazette*, April 1989, p.194, Table 24).

Why has there been an improvement? It is possible that shifts in levels of unemployment may result from changes in the willingness of groups to accept poor pay as a price of employment, or as a result of changes in the degree of dependence on the open labour market. And of course, some employers may have responded to a tightening labour market by drawing on pools of unemployed ethnic minority labour even though they continue to hold racist attitudes.

OTHER FORMS OF DISCRIMINATION

Older workers, people with disabilities, people with health problems and people with learning difficulties, all suffer the problem of discrimination. Their experience of discrimination results from being stereotyped, that is, not being treated as an individual with individual capacities. Employers rarely investigate the capacity of such individuals; instead they assume that their capacity to work is non-existent, or at least not worth its price in the labour market. Consequently, individuals in these groups form the pools of unemployed and the modern unemployables. There is evidence of higher unemployment rates amongst older workers. For example, in 1988 men aged 50 to 64 were more likely to be unemployed than those aged 25 to 49 (*Employment Gazette*, April 1989, p.192).

The exact magnitude of the unemployment problem experienced by people with health problems or a disability is not clear, but a survey of nearly 1000 people in Ealing during 1988 suggests that ill-health and disability is a major factor in the distribution of unemployment. The survey found that over a quarter of people without jobs on a sample of council estates had a health problem or a disability which restricted their activity inside or outside of their home (*The Ealing Skills Survey Report*, London Borough of Ealing, Planning and Economic Development, no date). Those with ill-health or a disability are certainly prone to unemployment: the Labour Force Survey for 1987 found that the unemployment rate of people who are limited in the kind of work they can do by a health problem or a disability was 23 per cent – two and a half times that for able bodied people (*Labour Market Quarterly Report*, January 1989, p.10). And Department of Employment figures for 1989 apparently show an even higher proneness: nearly 80 per cent of all disabled people who were of working age were unemployed, compared to a national average of 6 per cent. This situation does appear to be due in part to rejection by employers. For instance, a study of secretarial job hunting in London shows that for every four job applications by a disabled person, one will be turned down because of their disability (*Disability Now*, December 1989). For people with learning difficulties it has long been the case that only a small proportion of those with severe difficulties have been able to break into the labour market.

Will the fortunes of these groups change? In the late 1980s not even the demographic time bomb – the decline in school leavers – appeared to make any difference. For as we have already noted, there was no evidence from the 1989 Training Agency and NEDO survey that many employers were turning to disabled or older people because of difficulties in recruiting young workers.

THE STATE AND EQUAL OPPORTUNITIES

The state has failed in its educational role with respect to the realisation of equal rights. This is perhaps easiest to see in respect of the failure of employers to actually manage equal opportunity policies.

Take the case of equal opportunities for ethnic minorities. In 1984 a Code of Practice issued by the CRE came into force, which set out clearly what employers needed to do in managing equal opportunities. This has not proved sufficient to stimulate employers into action. A Tribunal case involving British Telecommunications PLC in 1985 revealed how lax even major employers were in this respect. The Tribunal was critical of a situation in which an official of the company responsible for short-listing job applicants was unable to point to any document stating the components of the equal opportunity policy, any measures to encourage applications for particular work from under-represented racial groups, and any monitoring of selection decisions.

The British Railways Board came in for very strong criticism in a Tribunal case heard in 1986. They were criticised by the Tribunal for what appeared to be a complete lack of relevant training of management staff and staff concerned with selecting employees for promotion. Thus they were not training them to avoid discrimination in their attitudes, nor were they training them to carry out their responsibilities and supervision. The Board was criticised for the lack of instruction which meant that company officials who gave evidence at the Tribunal were completely unaware of the contents of the Race Relations Act and the recently issued Code of Practice. It seems that these officials had not even received any written circulars or memoranda on racial discrimination and its avoidance.

The Tribunal underlined the serious view they took of the deficiencies exposed in British Railways management in the following words:

> we are perfectly at a loss to understand how it can be that in 1986, no less than 10 years after the Race Relations Act was introduced, they have not established an effective programme or programmes to deal with the matters which arise by reason of that Act. (*Employment Report*, Vol VII, No.3, November 1986, p.9)

The fact that the unemployment rate of ethnic minorities was double that of whites in 1985 may also be put down to the lack of action by employers. This is shown by a Marplan poll commissioned by the *Financial Times*, which was based on a sample of 505 company directors interviewed by telephone in October 1985. The poll found that less than one in five (18 per cent) had taken any steps in the last year or so to employ more members of the ethnic communities – four-fifths had done nothing at all (Brittan, 1985, p.36).

It is clear that the state has set out the rights of women, ethnic minorities, older people, disabled people, etcetera, to be equal but it has not taken steps which would ensure these rights could be enjoyed in practice. The question arises as to why it has failed to take them. The only answer can be that it has not been prepared to limit the liberty of others in society to discriminate. But since the liberty of any citizen is just the rights they have under the constitutional and legal framework, the liberty to discriminate actually means that the state has failed to restrict the rights of some groups to an extent which is compatible with equality for women, ethnic minorities, older people, and so on.

Until the state does organise the realisation of equality of employment opportunities, the British economy will continue to squander enormous human resources. In the meantime, the state's laws on equality of opportunity represent evidence that we have counterfeit laws and a counterfeit state.

Part II
Reforms

In the earlier chapters we examined the current problems, difficulties, and in a genuine sense the crises which attend the British labour market. As the world economy develops, with the emergence of strong Pacific Rim economies and the continued intense trading competition with economies inside the European Community, the crisis in the labour markets of Britain has been seen by policy makers as demanding efforts to overcome and make the British economy work more effectively.

Some of these efforts have been forthcoming from the state, which has sought to reform and reorganise education and training, and welfare and social security to support the working of the labour market (see Chapters 4 and 5). The state has also directly attempted to reform the trade union movement of Britain, and this can be linked to a diagnosis which attributed inflexibilities in the labour market to trade union action. Simultaneously, the unions were subjecting themselves to reform – pushed on by their experience of unemployment and by problems of equality within their own organisations. Both the state instigated and the self-induced trade union reforms are explored in Chapter 6. Finally, in Chapter 7 we explore the attempted reform of production, in which we have raised complex issues such as the growth of flexible working, 'Japanisation' and 'Post-Fordism'.

All these different institutional reforms (education and training, welfare and social security, trade unions and production) have been aimed at transforming the situation. It is an important point that these reforms were *attempts* at reform, and not the realisation of reform. In the event, the evidence suggests that they have been failed attempts to shore up that labour market. On the whole, they have not proved successful and have at times made things worse.

4 Education, Training and Industry

This book's main concern is to demonstrate the complexity of the social relationships of the labour market. And yet, even given that complexity, we are also committed to exploring the simplistic way in which various Government policies have simulated an understanding of that labour market. We are demonstrating that within the labour market, and within the lives and morality of the people that make up that market, it is not possible to assume that human activity can be turned into labour in an unproblematic way. People cannot be *made* into the commodity labour in the straightforward way steel can be shaped into cars and blank paper shaped into forms or letters.

We have pointed out the vitally important part played by different sets of social policies and human activities in the actual reconstruction of human activity into labour market activity. It is a paradox that a Government which believes such a market is a 'natural' phenomenon, which happens simply because of its inherent relationship with the world, should also be a Government which believes so powerfully in intervening in that labour market to make things happen. The particular 'natural' activity seems to need a great deal of policy assistance before it can be made to work properly. Given the complexity and difficulty of actually making the labour market work, it is not surprising (especially to those outside of a more simplistic economic policy) that there has been a considerable amount of social policy involved in those attempts.

Amongst the many activities that have attempted to fashion that relationship on a more secure basis, one of the most obvious and largest is that of the education system. It may appear to be a commonplace to state that any education system must have a set of labour market outcomes that are of the greatest importance to any economy. It may be an equal commonplace to expect that discussions about labour market needs would play a dominant role in the politics of education in any advanced capitalist society. In Britain, though, such a set of commonplaces have not been that common.

49

THE PAST 100 YEARS

In the 19th century Great Britain was the last industrialised country to introduce universal elementary education. This comparative tardiness was commented on at the time by all sections of society. Germany, France and the United States had introduced state education earlier and had done so very directly to provide an educated and skilled labour force for the future – although in Germany this was supplemented by the perceived need for an educated army. Britain's 'late development' is still working its way through our system and has been reproduced generation after generation. For that delay was not simply a matter of months, years and decades. The shape and form of the education system was made by a very wide variety of influences, only one of which was a direct labour market concern. Of greater and singular importance was the role of the education system in maintaining and recreating class inequalities. Elementary education was constructed within a system which restricted it to one class and ensured that others had secondary and higher education.

In 1867 Robert Lowe, who coined the wonderful phrase following male urban franchise in 1867, that 'It is absolutely necessary to compel our future masters to learn their letters', made this aim crystal clear. In arguing for the formation of elementary schools, the levying of a compulsory rate for their maintenance and also creating a law on compulsory attendance, he urged the complete overhaul of upper class education as well. The latter would teach the upper classes sufficiently well to 'know the things that working men know, only know them infinitely better in their principles and their details'. This knowledge would allow them to 'assert their superiority over the workers, a superiority assured by greater intelligence and greater civilisation'. It would ensure that the upper classes could 'conquer back by means of a wider and more enlightened cultivation some of the influence they have lost by political change'. It would also ensure that the upper classes would 'exhibit to the lower classes that higher education to which, if it were shown to them, they would bow down and defer' (Lowe, 1867, pp.9–10 and 32). As we shall see, the construction of an education system with sharp class divides has severe problems for a society that may also want to construct a modern labour force.

The proportion of British children who stayed on in education after reaching 16 years of age in 1989 was lower than that of any other industrialised country. The 42 per cent of Great Britain looks distinctly odd against the 75 per cent of Germany and the 95 per cent of

Singapore or South Korea. A chauvinism which dismisses 'foreign' post-16 education for its lack of quality stumbles against the fact that Britain has an even greater disparity at the age of 18, where we have a considerably lower proportion staying on. At every level of skill, beyond the basics, the British education system of the late 1980s produced significantly less people than any of our industrial competitors or indeed our non-competitors.

On the other hand, in 1986 the proportion of classic graduates from Oxford and Cambridge Universities to be employed by the Home Civil Service at its administrative officer level dipped below 50 per cent for the first time. This confirms that the elite of the civil service still believe that an understanding of Beowulf is more essential than anything else to the running of the modern state, and that they are perfectly happy to select one half of their membership from a pool that represents a small percentage of the total population.

At an international level development has been different. The politics of mass educational provision was firmly linked in most countries undergoing industrialisation with the improvement of labour skills and their availability in the market. The 'economy' and 'the market' were seen simply not to work without the social dimension of a policy of universal education. There were, and are, sophisticated arguments about how an education system can provide basic labour market skills to be complemented later on by a changing and much more specific training. In both capitalist and socialist countries such an analysis of education has been straightforward – plans and reforms have been implemented with this in mind.

In Britain the educational debate about universal education in mid Victorian England included much stronger strands of class inequality and social control. These debates, later complemented by the labour movement's political struggle for a greater equality of educational opportunity, have provided a much more directly 'political' background to educational reform. Both then and now, powerful class inequalities have directly overdetermined the economic debate, leading to a situation where the highest pinnacle of school qualifications is an 'A' level that has no recognised relationship with any form of economic development, and the most sought after higher education places are in subjects and institutions that are much more closely linked to the pre-industrial world than to the world of advanced technology.

It is therefore our contention that the politics of the 110 years of compulsory state education in this country is considerably more complex than simply linking educational structure and content and the needs of the labour market.

Political parties and social groups have had other agendas which have limited the success of the policy and practice of education from carrying out any labour market role – either a labour market role within the free market model of the right, or a labour market role within the planned social economy of the left.

As we shall see in the detail of the reforms of the 1980s, there is a sharp contradiction between the language and policy of labour market needs and the language and policy of school, college and university practice. Just some examples of the way in which this has developed in the last 100 years will provide an important backdrop to the successive failures of the British education system.

THE THIRTIES AND FORTIES: GOLD, SILVER AND BRONZE

Universal education beyond the age of 11 – that is education that was not considered 'elementary' – was also very late in coming to this country. The Education Acts of the 1870s and 80s made it clear that state schooling was to finish at the age of 11. At the turn of the century an alliance of the labour movement and major employers had illegally used the London School Board to build and maintain 'higher grade' schools for children past the age of 11. These met a ready need for longer training: a need argued for, constructed and paid for by London employers. However, the 1902 Education Act took those powers away and post-11 education for the working classes was put back a further 17 years.

In the 1920s and 30s though, the new local education authorities were committed, through reacting to local economic needs, to the development of a patchwork secondary system. At the end of the 1930s the Norwood Committee was set up to look into the development of a nationwide system for the 1940s. The war intervened, but their thinking was still published in 1943 and shaped the secondary system for a generation.

Norwood was the Headmaster of Harrow – an interesting choice to chair this committee since it represents the predominance over the nation of a particular class style and content of education. The public school system, whilst adequately reproducing a powerful elite to 'run the country' did not have a good record of producing people to run businesses or any aspect of the economy. Yet it was from this stock that 'educationists' were drawn.

The Report provided an extremely simple and 19th century economic analysis of the labour market, a social analysis of the nature of the British people and an educational analysis of existing public provision. Happily, all three of these realities actually fitted together to provide a relationship between class background, intelligence and schooling which would produce the three different sorts of people needed in the labour market.

There was, at the base, a great demand for unskilled labour which was met by boys and girls who could not reason for themselves and who liked repetitive tasks. The new Secondary Modern schools met these needs. In the middle were those technical and skilled tasks that were necessary to develop the economy and there was a group of boys and girls who were happiest in dealing with more technical but not abstract issues. The development of technical schools met these needs. Lastly the country needed a group of people who could deal with the world on an abstract plane. There were people that fitted into such a group and the old grammar schools could provide these needs. In one of the funniest state document statements of the 20th century Norwood explores this happy trinity of trinities developing the argument of how all three aspects fit together.

One of the major problems of educational theory and organisation has always been, and always will be, to reconcile diversity of human endowment with practical schemes of administration and instruction.... Our point is that rough groupings, whatever may be their ground, have in fact established themselves in general educational experience, and the recognition of such groupings in educational practice has been justified both during the education and in the after career of the pupils. For example, English education has in practice recognised the pupil who is interested in learning for its own sake, who can grasp an argument or follow a piece of connected reasoning, who is interested in causes... who cares to know how things came to be as well as how they are. Such pupils, educated by the curriculum commonly associated with the grammar school, have entered the learned profession or have taken up higher administrative or business posts. Again the history of technical education has demonstrated the importance of recognising the needs of the pupils whose interests and abilities lie markedly in the field of applied science and applied art. The boy [sic] in the group has a strong interest in this direction... he often has an uncanny insight into the intricacies of mechanisms whereas the subtleties of language construction are too delicate for him.

Again there has of late years been a recognition, expressed in the framing of the curriculum of still another grouping of occupations.

The pupil in this group deals more easily with concrete things than with ideas. He may have much ability, but it will be in the realm of facts. His mind must turn its knowledge or its curiosity to immediate test. This test is essentially practical. His horizon is near and within a limited area. His movment is generally slow. (Board of Education, 1943, pp.2–4)

The absence of any girls in these secondary schools must have alarmed the women who were learning some lessons about equality of sacrifice in the streets of Britain at that time. The report came out within two months of the battle of El Alamein, and did not receive widespread publicity from a Government that was fighting for democracy and equality.

The problem of actually *how* you sorted out these different groups of people was solved by the Spens Report which demonstrated that IQ tests at the age of 11 could act as predictors for these life long attributes (Board of Education, 1938). The 11-plus was born and the next 25 years of educational history was set.

One of the basic themes of this book is the puzzled way in which many Continental European commentators look at aspects of the British experience and its resistance to adaptation. It is not so much that other nations are *morally* committed to equality of opportunity or *economically* committed to a closer labour market relationship for education. They realise these associations have to be constructed over time. Their puzzlement is based upon the adherence, sometimes with great passion, of sections of the population in Britain to institutions that *only* seem to have their anachronism going for them. The tripartite secondary education system is one of them.

Much of this is indeed funny. The fact that Government then believed this, and that the bulk of educational experiences for millions of post-war children were constructed around this tripartite system does have a humorous side to it. This should not be allowed to confuse us about the disastrous consequences of such theories. The rigidity of analysis which tried to powerfully recreate the rigidity of a social class system completely cut across the necessity of movement that existed in the post war economy.

The British, as with other economies, needed a labour force that was convinced of its own capacity to move both socially and economically. To make these movements it was necessary to be able to 'learn' new things; develop new ideas and skills; to respond to new processes. It was imperative that people possessed intellectual and social confidence.

If several generations had been told and retold that what they could and could not do had been established by the time they were 11, and that the great majority of them were incapable of further education, then unfortunately millions believed it. An educational system constructed to meet the rigidities of a social class system could not suddenly meet the needs of an economy committed to movement and change.

THE SPLIT BETWEEN EDUCATION AND TRAINING IN FURTHER AND HIGHER EDUCATION

Historically, the further and higher education system in this country has also failed to create strong and dialectical links with the way in which the economy develops. On the one hand, as we have already mentioned, the pinnacle of academic success for a section of the state remains not a Masters in Business Administration, but a classics degree from Oxford or Cambridge. To obtain a place at either of these or other Universities students must take a qualification, the advanced level certificate, which is useful *only* for entry to higher education. If students take other qualifications that have a dual use – either as entry to higher education or as a vocational qualification in their own right, and should they want to enter University at 18, then a 'special case' has to be made out for them which will be argued separately case by case. Thus a student, her or his parents, a teacher and careers teacher would all learn that it would be odd to take a qualification at 16 which was at all vocationally orientated if they *may* want to go on to higher education. People who *may* want to obtain a degree at 21 or 22 must choose to be non-vocational at the age of 16. Thus the people who choose to be vocational at 16 do so in the knowledge that the 'really clever young people' are rejecting that path and are leaving a vocational education to those with less prospects and less expressed intelligence.

A wide variety of educational reforms and Governments have not only failed to tackle this but have ever more deeply enshrined this in educational experience. The expansion of higher education in the early 1960s, taking place under Conservative and Labour Governments, did so on the basis of 'A' level passes. The new polytechnic sector, growing in the late 1960s and early 1970s, did so on the basis of 'A' level entry to it. The Wilson–Callaghan Government continued expansion of higher education, and did so on the same basis despite, as we shall see, an emphasis on a debate with industry. Up until the end of 1989, the Thatcher Government, for all their commitment to industrial linkage, continued to insist on the normal route of entry being a specialised 'A' level.

EDUCATION AND INDUSTRY LINKS: THE DEBATE
BETWEEN 1975 AND 1990

So far we have explored how certain continuities in the ways in which education was organised up until the mid 1970s and 80s have been reconstructed with no real relationship to labour market needs. This section of the chapter will review recent attempts to change that and point out the very specific view of the labour market that has been contained in those attempts. However, before discussing either the recent changes brought about by the Conservative Government, or why the politics of education have been so complex over this whole period, we can best illustrate the nature of this debate by looking at the language that has been used in that debate over the last 15 years.

In 1975 a 'Great Debate' on education was launched by the Prime Minister Jim Callaghan in a speech at Ruskin College. It is interesting to note that the Labour Party had been re-elected at two elections in 1974 and that education had always been seen as a part of the successes of the Labour Party in both central and local government activity. Given this, it is significant that there should be any criticism at all of the education system by a Labour Prime Minister; for this was criticism of something that he and his party had played a major part in constructing. It is further significant that the criticism came from a new Prime Minister. If the Labour Party had been in charge nationally during seven of the last eleven years, if they had been in charge of most local education authorities for most of that period, and if the major reforms in education carried out in the previous ten years had happened as a result of Labour Party politics, why was there the need for the Prime Minister to initiate a critical Great Debate? Why not celebrate what was there?

The debate was initiated by and was to continue to take place between the education system and sources *outside*. It was aimed at raising the question at the core of this chapter – the problematic relationship between the education system and the labour market. The problematic was to be constructed within the overall problem of a decline in international competitiveness. The debate posed labour market issues within this wider economic problem, demonstrating that people do not 'naturally' join the labour market. Young people who completed education, be they successful or unsuccessful, were not 'made ready' for the labour market in any coherent way. The debate opened that question. As such we would mark that moment as a change in the nature of the work–education relationship in this country. However, the simplicity of the solutions that have been put forward over this period also demonstrates the infancy of the way in which educators in this country understand and become involved in this relationship.

THEIR PERCEPTION OF THE PROBLEM

The 1977 Green Paper on the education system accepted the same problematic that we do:

> It is vital to Britain's economic recovery and standard of living, that the performance of manufacturing industry is improved and that the whole range of government policies, including education, contribute as much as possible to improving industrial performance and thereby increasing industrial wealth. (DES Green Paper, 1977, para. 1.16)

It is interesting to note that such a statement was made as a part of a Great Debate, rather than being simply an axiomatic statement about social and economic needs of an advanced society. Also interesting is that even though it came from a party committed to the view that labour is the source of wealth, this valuing of labour as the core of national wealth production was met by much of that party with a storm of protest.

Most teachers and people involved in education felt that the debate posed the question about the purposes of education in a far too limited economic way. The protest demonstrated the extent to which the Labour Party was bound up with a particular experience of education, seen as separate from the nature of work and the labour market. The powerful view of education as aimed at 'personal development' or as being 'an activity in its own right' held and still holds many educators (teachers and administrators) in its thrall. For many this view is posed in opposition to the development of labour market policies and the development of improved market positions for young people who have an education and have qualifications.

Having identified the issue though, the detail of the problem as to why the education–labour market relation was not working was discussed very schematically. The nature of the problem was raised in 1975, and the form of its solution became set in the mid 1970s in such a way as to provide the powerful, and we believe deeply mistaken, ideological ground for the next 15 years.

In 1974 a major survey of employers' reactions to young workers was carried out. In this, employers complained that young people 'questioned' and tended to resent guidelines about their appearance; moreover, it seems 'a large number of unemployed young people...have attitudes which...are not acceptable to employers and act as a hindrance to young people in securing jobs' (National Youth Employment Council, 1974, pp.29 and 74).

The line of reasoning went like this. The large-scale problem was one of a lack of economic performance. This was caused by problems with labour, which were in some way connected with the attitudes of young people. Young people had just been to school and had therefore been placed in this questioning frame of mind by all that had been going on in school. Schools themselves, especially primary schools, had been through a process of change which seemed to involve them in teaching more about problem solving rather than respect for authority. We could conclude, therefore, that the seat of the problem experienced in the British economy was caused by the increased questioning of an education system.

Callaghan identified the problem by saying that there was 'no virtue in producing socially well adjusted members of society who are unemployed because they do not have skills' (TES, 22 October 1976). Looking back on this quote it was rather surprising that no-one questioned whether the education system was actually turning out 'socially well adjusted people' at the time. The popular media were developing stories about football hooligans and the punk revolution was not far away. The level of civic education and health education may well have been better by the mid-1970s than it had been before, but all the surveys carried out then and now demonstrate that young people left school both democratically and personally ignorant.

Whether schools were socially successful or not, it was the education system's economic failures that were being highlighted. The economic failure was seen to be caused by this supposed stress on, and success in, meeting *social needs*.

The previous year the MSC had made the argument clearly:

In recent years the social environment in a number of schools with more emphasis on personal development and less on formal instruction, has been diverging from that which is encountered in most work situations, where the need to achieve results in conformity with defined standards and to do so within a fixed time limit calls for different patterns of behaviour. The contrast is more marked where changes in industrial processes have reduced the scope for individual action and initiative. (MSC, 1975, p.15)

Here the lines for the debate were drawn. The analysis of the workplace was that it needed more people who think less; who could carry out tasks by rote; and who were not interested in personal development. Indeed this analysis went further and claimed that more people who think less were needed in the mid-1970s than were needed before. The education system was viewed as encouraging questioning and personal development and as devaluing rote learning. Therefore, there was a mismatch.

The argument we are developing in this book agrees that there was a mismatch but fundamentally questions *both of the assumptions*. The world of work in 1975 (and even more so in 1990) needed a much higher level of self-motivation and self-driven activity than before. In the words of the MSC, it provided considerably greater scope for individual action and initiative, and not less. It also needed people who had the confidence and capacity to learn to change very easily and very quickly. Teaching people by rote could not achieve these labour market skills nor confidence in the ability to relearn.

Whilst there was some evidence that by 1975 primary schools had developed a more self-expressive attitude to learning, the secondary education system still had as its pinnacle of learning a system of teaching and administration which did not reward self-expression and learning. Studies over the last 15 years have shown the way in which the last years of secondary school and the experience of an examinations led system leaves a very large number of young people, if not a majority, with little opportunity to gain confidence and raise their level of individual action and initiative (Corrigan, 1979; Willis, 1977). The mismatch was there but by no means in the direction of the analysis.

Equally absent was any social analysis of the world that young people were growing up in outside of school and work. The hours spent in school could affect people's educational capacity, but the hours spent out of school also played a significant role. The analysis of the impact of education on work has always found that a difficult concept to take on board. Not only was it not noticed how different was that world outside school, but it seemed not to matter. Since the debate was launched by the Prime Minister and since the state 'controlled' education, then that must be where the blame lay. However, that is the way in which the great debate was set up. A belief that the world of work was boring and that school was making it seem too interesting and self-directed.

It was into this confusion that successive governments pumped considerable numbers of policy initiatives. The confusion could be found not only inside the ideas of each policy but in the different departments of state that produced the initiatives. The beginning of the 1990s saw the Department of Education and Science (DES) developing business awareness as a cross curriculum theme in the National Curriculum. The DES was also heavily involved in the encouragement of employers to fill at least one place on every school board of governors and to form a majority of places on every college of further education and public sector higher education institution board of governors.

The Department of Trade and Industry, with its Enterprise in Education initiative, has pledged to find work experience placements for 10 per cent of all teachers annually and to ensure that employers play a full role in the governance of schools and colleges.

The Department of Employment has been financing the careers service in schools since 1972, developing the Technical and Vocational Education Initiative since 1982 and funding some 20 per cent of public sector further education through Training Agency money.

The involvement of three of the large departments of state in developing a coherent policy for partnership between the labour market and schools and further education is almost certainly not a good sign. The fact that two of them have little traditional relationship with schools is also likely to cause some confusion.

Given the way in which this debate has been formed, some of this confusion may be inevitable. It is, however, likely that the debate would have succeeded in moving slightly further forward if the issue had been simply that of an education–labour market mismatch. For most of the last 15 years though it has been overlayed by the powerful reality of massive, structural and large scale, youth unemployment. Whilst the debate may have started with the failure of a liberal education system to meet the needs of a capitalist economy, it continued as a debate about what to do for the millions of young people who left school without a job. There could be no real debate about ideological and social mismatch between education and employment when for very many young people there was no employment. Therefore, whilst the period 1975–1990 saw the creation of a string of post school training schemes to deal with this problem, the real problem that they have been aimed at has been structural youth unemployment.

YOUTH UNEMPLOYMENT AND YTS

In his excellent study on YTS, Dan Finn says:

> By 1986 more than half of under 18 year olds and a quarter of under 25 year olds were unemployed....There were over 300 000 young adults who had never had a job since leaving school. It was these realities, and the quality of many YTS places, not young people's alleged idleness, which were seriously undermining the credibility of the scheme, and provoking the different reactions of young people to it. (Finn, 1987, p.187)

In October 1975 the Job Creation project was set up, followed by the Work Experience Programme in 1976. These were replaced by the Youth Opportunities Programme in April 1978, which was planned to accommodate 240 000 youngsters. This programme consisted of work preparation courses and work experience. The Manpower Services Commission (MSC) saw the new two-year YTS as 'not about taking people out of the labour market but was designed to "put people in" on terms that would secure them entry' (MSC, 1984). In 1987 nearly six out of ten of the whole 16–17 year old age group were meant to be participating in the two year YTS. As with the Ruskin speech ten years earlier, the ideological problem was clear. The two year scheme was meant to give young people practical skills for finding jobs and the kinds of attitudes that will make them useful and employable.

There was however something difficult at the core of these schemes. They had sprung from an analysis which was based upon a recognition that the education system was failing to prepare people for a labour market. Yet they led to schemes that were primarily designed to keep people out of that labour market since it was failing badly to provide very many jobs at all. As a consequence, such schemes have been less interested in developing a better relationship between the labour market and education and more interested in keeping young people off the dole and off the streets.

THE STATE AND TRAINING

These schemes were largely organised by the Manpower Services Commission (MSC), set up in the 1970s, and which towards the middle of the 1980s was turned into the Training Commission (TC), finishing that decade as the Training Agency (TA). The total expenditure on vocational education and training by the MSC/TC/TA expanded enormously after the mid-1970s. In 1974–5 the expenditure amounted to 96.4 million pounds (318.5 million pounds at 1988 prices); this rose to 1613 million pounds in 1987–8 (*Employment Gazette*, May 1989, p.265). As the money spent by the state on vocational education and training went up, so did the numbers who were involved in the state's youth and adult training. This is shown in Table 1.

Table 1 Numbers of people on MSC/TC training schemes

Year	Adult training	YOP/YTS
1979–80	110 538	216 400
1980–81	111 468	360 000
1981–82	102 696	553 000
1982–83	85 250	543 000
1983–84	109 850	353 979
1984–85	131 800	395 000
1985–86	269 650	404 000

Source: *Employment Gazette*, April 1987, p.214.

Despite the massive increase in public sector training facilities since 1960, employers in the private sector had remained the most important providers of training. According to a survey carried out for the Training Agency, private and public employers spent a total of 18 billion pounds on training in the year 1986–7, which, included 11 billion pounds spent by private employers, and far exceeded the amount spent by the state on education and training (*Employment Gazette*, May 1989, p.265; Training Agency, no date). Moreover, the Government had no intention of taking over the main responsibility for funding training. This was made plain by Norman Fowler, Secretary of State for Employment, in a Government White Paper in 1988. He said:

> we must invest in the skills and knowledge of our people and build up industry's skill base, through a strategy of training through life, to enable Britain to continue to grow and to generate jobs. The prime responsibility for this investment lies with employers. (Employment Department, 1988, p.4)

Whilst private employers were assigned the function of investing in the skills and knowledge of the British people, the Thatcher Government made it quite clear that it had a duty to influence the level and quantity of training. The White Paper's very existence and substance testified to the Government's concern not to leave training entirely to the discretion of private employers. The Secretary of State wrote in the preface to it:

> The White Paper sets out an agenda for action starting now and developing through the next decade. It concentrates in particular on training, and on the need to set forward-looking training policies not just for young people but for everyone throughout their working lives. (Employment Department, 1988, p.3)

At about the same time as the White Paper was published, the importance of the Government intervening to influence the training activities of employers was being underlined by the CBI's Industrial Trends Survey of manufacturing (see Table 2). This showed that as many as one in four British companies were expecting their output to be limited by skill shortages (NIER, August 1989, p.90). The wide extent of the skill shortages problem was corroborated by other survey evidence. The service sector was experiencing difficulties in recruiting clerical staff, construction was short of bricklayers, carpenters and plasterers in some parts of the country, and widespread shortages were uncovered by the fifth annual Skills Survey conducted by the CBI on behalf of the Training Agency in November 1988. This last survey, which obtained responses from 938 firms, showed that nearly one in two of the firms had not been able to meet their skill needs and a reported 45 per cent of them said that production had been affected in the last year by a shortage of skilled labour. Occupations reported to be in shortage included professional engineers, machinists, computer and management services staff, maintenance electricians, sales staff and professional financial personnel (*Labour Market Quarterly Report*, May 1989, p5).

The crisis implied by the scale of these shortages was hard to reconcile with the fact that the seasonally adjusted unemployment figures for the United Kingdom were showing just over two million people unemployed in December 1988. An economy still in the grip of mass unemployment was still suffering severe problems of skill shortages. To some extent the skill shortage problem was a manifestation of the economic recovery since skill shortages had almost disappeared in 1980 and 1981.

Table 2   Percentage of firms expecting skilled labour shortages to limit output: CBI Industrial Trends Survey of manufacturing

Survey date (October)	Percentage expecting output to be limited
1978	27
1979	20
1980	4
1981	3
1982	3
1983	6
1984	8
1985	15
1986	12
1987	19
1988	28

Source: *National Institute Economic Review*, No.129, August 1989, p.90.

YTS AND SKILL TRAINING

Given the reemergence of large scale skill shortages once unemployment fell below 2 million, what had the expenditure on YTS and Employment Training for adults achieved? Whilst in theory YTS was meant to be about providing young people with a combination of broad foundation training and training for occupational competency, in practice there was confusion about exactly what level of vocational training it fitted. In some industries YTS was actually used by employers to exploit public funds to carry out the first part of apprenticeship training. In other cases, critics denied that there was any vocational training at all, and suggested that the scheme was being used to bring down pay levels of young people.

It is certain that the scheme provided a wide variety of training experiences. In some cases, training managers 'topped up' the MSC levels of expenditure to provide high quality education and training. In some cases it provided pre-vocational training. In other cases it could well have overlapped with apprenticeship training. At its best YTS could have been helping to equip Britain with an adaptable and flexible workforce which was receptive to further training and retraining to meet ever-changing circumstances and opportunities. However, experience of YTS in the 1980s provided little basis for optimism that YTS was providing this high quality level of training.

Firstly, the YTS record on producing vocational qualifications was poor – even when it became a two year scheme.

> Under one year YTS around 20 per cent of leavers gained a qualification. In 1987/88 29 per cent gained a qualification. Latest survey results in the twelve month period ended August 1988 shows 36 per cent gaining qualifications. (*Labour Market Quarterly Report*, May 1989, p.15)

From a Government committed to 'value for money' this level of failure would have been expected to raise severe problems for the continuation of the expenditure.

Secondly, an examination of the actual skills being acquired under YTS compares very unfavourably with the results of the mass vocational training system in West Germany. This was precisely the point made by Daly et al. (1985) in their study of the metal-working trades in the two countries:

> When YTS is combined, as it will be in the next few years, with the benefits of an increased technological element in schooling (through the Technical and Vocational Education Initiative), it may well serve to raise the proficiency of the unskilled section of the labour force to an adequate level; but much more will be necessary if at least some proportion of the workforce is to be raised to the higher skill

standards implicit in the German vocational scheme. (Daley et al, 1985, p.60)

Steedman and Wagner, who looked into the clothing industry, found that two thirds of the practical skills mastered over two years on the YTS were mastered by West German trainees in the first two months of their course (Steedman and Wagner, 1989). Finally, Jarvis and Prais made the following comment on YTS training for retail occupations: 'YTS courses may lead to a variety of qualification, almost all hitherto – that is, under the one-year YTS arrangements – below anything that would be recognised in France or Germany as a 'vocational qualification' (1989, p.61).

Thirdly, the administration of the scheme inspired little confidence in the overall competence with which the system had been organised. Thus there were reports in the media in August 1989 which referred to concerns that a quarter of the places on the Youth Training Scheme had not been filled – even though the managing agents had received the public money for providing the training.

These major faults in the scheme stem from its basic premise. Whilst Ministers continued to insist that the YTS scheme was in fact one of high quality training, the suspicion remained that it was primarily interested in removing young people from the dole queues and off the labour market. This suspicion was confirmed in the Autumn of 1989. The Secretary of State for Employment, in the statement on future public expenditure of that year, *cut* the amount spent on training because the level of unemployment had come down so much. The fact that the skills shortages in the early 1990s were universally agreed to be worse than before might have led to an increase in the training budget. However if 'training' is simply about stopping young people from being on the unemployment register then they were correct to cut it.

THE COUNTERFEITING OF SKILLED LABOUR

Ultimately, the Government's approach stemmed from a lack of appreciation of the importance of skill in the labour process, and therefore the importance of training. Successful vocational training systems, such as that found in West Germany, are based on the state organising the basic components of instruction, testing and certification into a system that works. This means more than success at fulfilling a narrow and essentially limited view of training, according to which training providers equip workers with the minimum necessary level of competence to enable them to do a specific job or production operation. Success should be measured by the degree to which 'skill' in a more comprehensive sense is achieved. A worker with skill in this more integral sense is one who is prepared to relate to their present and future work with some empowerment and flexibility: who has skills and knowledge which can be applied in situations which are dynamic, and who has skills which are in training parlance 'transferable'. It is such workers who are now needed to work in technologically advanced factories and workplaces (notwithstanding the counter-tendencies which have reduced skill requirements in some workplaces, for example, modern supermarkets).

The YTS arrangements for instruction of trainees was deficient. Under YTS there was often only workplace instruction. This was so even where trainees gained qualifications, as in the case of retailing. In the West German system of vocational training, instruction includes both workplace instruction and vocational *schooling* through three-year day release courses.

The arrangements for testing skill development were also deficient. Firstly, YTS was often operated without proper standards which could be tested; Daly et al, for example, commented on the 'lack so far of any examinable standards to be worked to under that scheme must limit its value in raising the technological capability of the workforce' (1985: p.60). Secondly, later moves to certify skill standards attained by YTS trainees were marred by the reliance on internal examination procedures. This was the case, for example, in retailing.

A very basic qualification in Retail Distribution Skills (City and Guilds course no. 9441) was obtained by some 2300 persons in Britain in 1986. The intention of this qualification was to meet employers' needs for a reliable certificate confirming that an applicant for employment already has an acquaintance with basic sales skills. It is usually attained by new entrant in nine months on the basis of brief part-time instruction on practical skills while at work (for example, during half-hour sessions on Thursday mornings plus one full day's off-the-job instruction; no attendance at college is required...

The candidate has to carry out ten specified basic practical tasks, such as using the telephone, restocking shelves, handling payments (including cheques and credit cards) and 'handling complaints'... no commodity-knowledge is called for, and no written work has to be produced. The completion of these tasks is signed for by someone accredited by the employer's designated training supervisor – a person not required to hold any formal qualifications – whose assessment techniques may, or may not, be 'moderated' by City and Guilds.

There is also a final written test of an hour's duration, externally set by City and Guilds, with fifty multiple-choice questions...

These multiple-choice questions are also marked by the training supervisor; if the candidate attends a college, a teacher may do the marking. (Jarvis and Prais, 1989, pp.64–5)

The practice in French and West German vocational training systems used external examination. Jarvis and Prais say with respect to the higher level vocational qualification in retailing (CAP): 'Also noteworthy is the French requirement of objective external assessment by examiners who do not know the candidates' (1989, p.62). Assessment of trainees by external persons (that is, not by their supervisors or teachers) was also operated in the German system; apprentices have written external examinations, and, for example, in the case of technical apprentices in woodworking there are also externally examined practical trade tests which last some 12 hours.

Even from the point of view of employers' recruitment decisions, external examination may be seen as providing a more useful qualification. Where there is an external assessment the system is inevitably less parochial and less tied to the requirements of the specific employer with whom the trainee is placed. Moreover, Jarvis and Prais were told by some employers that the City and Guilds system was 'open to abuse'; consequently they were not prepared to hire someone purely on the basis of this certificate, thereby undermining the nature of the qualification.

A more serious defect of internal examination, especially when combined with exclusive reliance on workplace instruction by supervisors (and thus no day-release schooling), is that the system is unlikely to raise itself above the provision of the most basic competence in specific skills needed for the specific work being undertaken. In other words, the individual trainee becomes competent at specific work of use in that setting, but does not attain skill which will make them a flexible resource capable of working under a variety of conditions in different workplaces and in different employments.

The growth in the proportion of YTS trainees who gained qualifications under these conditions did not provide a useful measure of the movement of the workforce towards the skilled flexible workforce required in the efficient and productive economy of the late 20th century. The rapid growth in qualifications instead measured the progress of skilled labour counterfeiting by the publicly organised system of training. The 'progress', such as it was, was simply explained by the financial inducement of public subsidy.

The introduction of National Vocational Qualifications did nothing towards making this counterfeiting impossible. This was demonstrated by the experiences of the retail industry and the introduction at the end of the 1980s of a new introductory vocational qualification – the Retail Certificate. The National Council for Vocational Qualifications (NCVQ) gave its approval in September 1988, and YTS subsidy was made dependent on the new qualifications from early 1989. In many ways this vocational training resembles the City and Guilds course referred to above. Training focuses on practical tasks such as handling payments, replenishing stock, manipulating sales displays, and using the telephone. And assessment is entirely internal – in the workplace and by the trainee's supervisor.

The counterfeiting of skilled labour consists of describing instructions in very basic skills as 'training', internal rating by supervisors as 'assessment' or 'testing', and the end result as a 'qualification'. Anybody who is new in a simple job receives instructions from their supervisor on how to do it, and is watched by that supervisor to see if they perform to an adequate standard. Producing this set of processes as if they equated to proper training is the process of counterfeiting.

The counterfeiting of goods is a well recognised phenomenon in world markets. It is a widely condemned practice. It involves the passing off of low quality goods as higher quality more expensive ones. It involves deception because customers believe they are acquiring 'originals', that is goods of high quality.

Britain in the 1980s witnessed a growing trend in the counterfeiting of another kind of commodity, one which has not been widely recognised, the counterfeiting of skilled labour. And it was done under the superintendance of the British state – by Thatcherism.

It also involved deception. The customers – employers – were not all deceived by the value of the qualifications that were being produced under YTS. But another party was also being deceived – labour itself. Not all labour. But those young people who took the qualifications as evidence of their skill. Perhaps fortunately for them, this deception was likely to go unnoticed for as long as they did not try to get a job with some firm where ideas of skill levels were more like those of the West Germans. Indeed, the British economy has become so uniformly a low skill, low pay economy, and the hegemony of amateurism and getting by is so strong, that such an encounter is unlikely.

Yet there is a price for this counterfeiting. That price will be paid by British society. The debasement of skill shows up in poor international productivity and thus poor economic performance. It is therefore a form of counterfeiting that deceives nobody in the long run – the goods just do not sell. But in the short run, the political-customer, the British citizen, is deceived into thinking that we have a vocational training system.

Unless YTS can be turned into a proper system of vocational training for Britain, history will have to write it off as a political expedient to deal with high unemployment. By 1988 YTS had 'soaked up' 16 per cent of 16 to 18 year olds; and only 10 per cent were unemployed. What would the unemployment figure have been without YTS?

ORGANISING TRAINING NOW

The current State strategy for training envisaged in *Employment for the 1990s* hinges on the state giving business leaders a more active role in training. The key organisational instrument of this strategy is the network of Training and Enterprise Councils, which are local bodies led by top private sector managers, and which are charged with spending public money on training unemployed and young people. They will subcontract training to local providers.

Other training, particularly that for employees in employment, remains a private sector concern and is continuing to be paid for out of private capital. If the Training and Enterprise Councils prove to be a successful device for increasing the commitment of business leaders to investment in training, then the experiment will deliver, maybe, increased total expenditure on training. It may also lead to business leaders actively organising more cost effective training.

But the strategy may be regarded as a high risk one. Our main European partners – Germany and France – have not adopted laissez-faire routes to meeting their training needs. The West Germans have a system of obligatory day-release at college for virtually all under 18s not in full-time education. And the French have a training levy on all employers. What will happen if the TECs do not tackle the root problem? What if the employers remain indifferent to training? Training cannot be left to the whim of the private sector. Rampant competition and the associated social system has brought Britain to its parlous economic state. Something has to be done to get labour valued.

Some employers favour the idea of a voucher system under which all employees would have a training entitlement. This circumvents the problem of some firms 'poaching' skilled workers without themselves adding to the supply through training – a paramount concern for many employers. It is also politically acceptable to those who want to see some decisive intervention into the training mess, but do not want a centralised system of state planning. Whether this idea will gather support and be taken up as a new state policy on training remains to be seen.

We have had 15 years of complex experimentation in youth training, combined with a continuous plethora of different schemes from three different ministeries to better relate education and employment. However, in the early 1990s the problem of the relationship between school, training and employment was joined by the problem of an increase in demand for labour combined with a downturn in supply of teenagers. Perhaps the passing of the conditions which led the state to devise schemes to keep young people off the dole queue will enable fresh and progressive thinking about education and training. However, for as long as the educational problem is posed as being an educational system which teaches people to think too freely for a labour market that essentially needs people to cope with a boring and unthinking level of work, there will be little movement forward.

5 Welfare and Social Security – The Construction and Reconstruction of the Labour Market

INTRODUCTION: WHY IS SOCIAL SECURITY POLICY RELEVANT?

Given the importance of wages and salaries as a major component of the world of work, it is necessary to understand the relevance of other forms of payment in society. Within a pure market model the simple logic is this. If people only go to work for money and if they can get that money from another source, then it is inevitable that they will not go to work. Whilst such a simple logic would not be followed by anyone, there has been a significant and prolonged impact of its rationale on a broad range of policies and culture.

If the ideology which dominates people's relationship to work is that a workforce will only work for wages, then wages and other forms of remuneration become the important linchpin of all labour market policy. The logic is simple and direct, if people work only for wages then the other forms of remuneration will detract from the willingness to work. As we shall see, Government's policies in recent years have increasingly underlined the singular importance of payment for work (as well as a range of other activities). Consequently there has been continual attention to how people who would otherwise work obtain other sorts of money.

It is significant though, that certain forms of remuneration have not been greatly affected by government policy – or at least they have not been greatly curtailed. If you already own a great deal of money you can live off the interest from that money and not have to go out to

72

work. If you own land or property, you can also gain income from rent and not have to work for money. If you are bequeathed money, or can sell some property, you may gain sufficient income to not have to work for money. Under these circumstances the supposed disincentive effect of being able to obtain alternative sources of income rather than from work does not seem to matter. Yet given the effect of the property market on upper middle class wealth in the South-East of England, it is likely that there will now be many families with a significant level of wealth, which could well lead to an early withdrawal from the labour market, a move into part time work, or in the case of children who are left a considerable amount of money from property, a refusal to ever enter that market.

In the late 18th and early 19th centuries, the class of people who could afford to live off of the income generated from their wealth were the object of considerable attack from egalitarians. Their fate in France was straightforward – either re-education or the guillotine. In this country the early socialists attacked the ability of these few to eat without working, calling them, at best, parasitical (Stedman Jones, 1986). Chartism kept its roughest attacks for such people. The early working class movement felt it was morally wrong to be able to live off an income which did not involve work.

In terms of contemporary analysis of social structure, it would only be a major economic issue for labour market analysis if the existing stocks of wealth, property and money were distributed more equitably throughout society. If this were the case then these forms of income may well have a significant effect upon whether numbers of people enter paid labour or not. However, since only a small proportion of people own sufficient wealth to generate income for them to live off, this only affects a small proportion of the population. It is a vital political and social matter – but does not materially affect millions of people's possibility to gain income in the present.

The single most important source of income apart from wages and profits is from the state social security system. In 1989, some 19 per cent of households were totally dependent on social security payments and 30 per cent were partially dependent. For over 150 years, Government's have been aware of the way in which social security systems potentially and actually interact with the wages system, and much of this chapter will be concerned with how the relationship has unfolded over that period. Initially though it is important to stress some of the problems that arise for a society that has its hegemonic form of income coming from wages and profits.

A WAGES ECONOMY AND A SOCIAL SECURITY SYSTEM: THE BASIC PROBLEM

The most simple problem for a wages-based income system is that the level of wages are constructed by a very wide range of market factors. People get paid a 'value' for a job which is derived from their relationship to labour market factors.

One word processor operator in a firm will receive similar amounts to another. They will both receive less than the programmer, who will receive a similar amount to another programmer. All will receive more than the cleaner of their room who will receive the same as a cleaner of every other room in the building. If one of the cleaners has a significantly greater set of material needs than the programmer, this is completely immaterial to the way in which the wages system works. If word processor operators suddenly change their lives and change the amount of needs that they have – this has no effect upon their wage level. If the firm suddenly increases overtime and their wages increase by 30 per cent, this has no relationship to changes in need. If the firm has to cut back on its wages bill and only provides short-term working, the workforce have to work out what to do with their existing level of need.

Since we have lived within a wage economy for such a considerable time, such a set of relationships may appear obvious. Given the past 200 years of history, it is impossible to imagine the world of work being about anything else. They *are* what the world of work is about. A wide range of different theories try to explain these wage differentials and similarities. Only one of them has taken any sort of conception of 'need' into account and this has been deeply ideological rather than material.

There has been an important analysis of how wages for men have been seen to need to support a family and those for women have not. The differentials between gender rates of pay have been ensured that 'men's wages' have been higher than women's wages. Of course this is no direct relationship to need – a man who is a second earner to a well paid female partner does not earn less than his fellow single earner because of it. A woman who is the sole earner in a family does not get paid a 'family wage'. Given the extent of women's involvement in the labour force, the notion of a man's wage equalling family wages is not a material issue but an ideological one. It allows men to be paid more than women and has no direct relationship with need. Largely then, within the way in which the wage economy distributes income, there is little concept of need. It is inconceivable that workers who did the same job would receive different amounts of money because their personal circumstances would be different. The rate for the job governs both sides of the wages bargain.

If other aspects of society were based in any way upon a recognition of need in the delivery of remuneration, then it is inevitable that there would be some clash between that set of institutions and the wages system. Much of the politics of the last century and a half has been based upon this clash. For persistently throughout this period there have been institutions and sets of social relationships which have always followed up the importance of need as a method of distributing income. For example, at different times in that 150 year history a variety of religions has often felt it was imperative to provide some resources to people simply because they needed it. Charity has been through a wide range of different methods of working – but some of it has always been a straightforward response to need.

The politics of the labour movement has ensured that some aspects of government, both central and local, has organised its services that way. A great deal of the way in which families relate one to another is based upon a recognition of need, and many local communities have persistently seen the world in that way and felt it was important to help those in need.

There is therefore a contradiction of historical importance in the systems of income provision within our society. Whilst the wage economy remains the hegemonic method of distributing resources, and most people would agree that if people want to improve their standard of living they should individually 'work harder', it is significant that most people would also feel that people in need should receive resources from the community. This may be described as a 'balance' between two different systems of remuneration – but in fact in a broad set of instances it exists as a contradiction – as a clash – between different ways of distributing society's resources. It is significant that the history of the last 150 years demonstrates that these two different philosophies cannot simply coexist (Gough, 1979).

If a system of social security has been created which provides remuneration for need, those who argue for wage economy cannot simply allow that to exist side by side with that economy. They claim that unless this is changed it will undermine the provision for need, and then the wages economy cannot work. For 150 years they have cried: 'Why should people work if they can live on relief or on the dole?' They have argued that if people can obtain remuneration out of work that is greater than in work, then wage rates go up, discipline at work falls and motivation disappears.

Some have gone further and argued that a social security system that provides levels of benefit which relate to need has had a crippling effect upon the whole British economy. Monetarist economists have argued that levels of benefit set the basic wage rates in society by providing a place for people to hide from the necessary distribution relationships of the labour market. The whole economy is undermined if people are paid by need by social security and paid by their market relationship at work. The wages system then, within this ideology, cannot 'peacefully coexist' with a social security system based upon need. It must fight to be universal if it is to be successful.

In recent years this clash has been at the core of Thatcherite policy and – as we shall see later in this chapter – need and the market have not sat happily together within this Government. Whilst the clash between wages for labour and payment based on need has not been particularly harsh in recent years, it has, as we have suggested, been involved in British politics throughout the last 150 years.

THE 1834 POOR LAW

In any book on the British labour market the role of the 1834 or 'new' Poor Law is of very great significance. It demonstrates more than any other single piece of legislation the interrelatedness of the labour market, political power and social security. Without the economic, social and cultural work of the new Poor Law the development of the whole British economy could have been profoundly different.

By the 1830s two related comprehensive historical trends had developed. On the one hand the new urban industrial economy had created a considerable demand for labour within towns and cities. Such a demand could not be met by the existing urban population, nor, given the conditions of life and death in the towns, from the immediate projected internal growth of that urban population (Engels, 1969). The shortage of an urban population was pushing wage rates up above the level that the new system of manufacture could afford. Labour would have to be imported from the countryside.

The growth of population in the early 19th century combined with new systems of farming to ensure that there was a surplus of labour within the countryside. However, despite the dislocations of the

Napoleonic Wars, most families had lived in the same area for generations. The notion of simply 'moving to the towns' was not an easy or attractive one. Contemporary songs demonstrate the rural view of urban life (From Hull and Halifax and Hell good Lord deliver me), not simply because of the material lives of ordinary people but because of the completely different and unknown life style. The 'simple' working of the labour market, where labour would move from unemployment to employment, did not work. It was stopped by culture.

It was also blocked by what was left of the waning power involved in the second major historical trend – the power of the ownership of land and agriculture. For a considerable period of time there had been a clash between the growing merchant and industrial powers in the country and the older powers of land. Whilst both of these political camps had their internal contradictions, with, for example, a growth within the countryside of capitalist farming techniques, the older landed interests wanted to keep their surplus of labour in the countryside to provide a pool of cheap labour and also to demonstrate their continued acendancy.

The new urban industrial power could not grow without that labour. There were within the one nation, and putting it at its crudest, two entirely different systems of labour market distribution which also had different social security systems.

Within the countryside, varieties of social security systems had emerged which were based partly upon the recognition of the needs of individuals and families. It must be stressed that these were the responsibility of the local parish vestry. Thus there were almost as many social security schemes as there were parishes within the locality. For many of these schemes it was necessary to have been born within the parish to benefit (Rose, 1972).

The most famous of these, the Speenhamland system, provided a subsidy to every family that was based upon the average price of bread and the size of the family. Thus expensive bread and a large family would provide a large weekly income, no dependents and a low price of bread would provide a small income. If the person was working and their wages were less than their 'needs', as calculated above, then their wages would be subsidised. Under these circumstances it would be possible for the local employer to pay low wages when she/he was employing people and also keep a large local pool of labour when there was no demand for labour. Eligibility for the continued receipt of benefit depended upon staying in the parish you were born in.

Consequently, it is very unlikely that people would move away from
such a scheme. Thus the geographical mobility of labour was impeded.

The local nature of eligibility and organisation, the rural base and
the provision of benefit in relationship to need, *all* demonstrate the
extent to which this particular network of social security systems met
the needs of those who gained their power from the land. The new
urban bourgeoisie, however, were not receiving sufficient labour
because of the immobility brought about by the system – nor did
such a system mesh with their wages system in the new industrial
setting. Whilst they could enforce a social security system within the
urban parishes that was more in line with that system of income
distribution, they were unable to enforce such a system through the
country as a whole. Consequently they were still short of labour.

These two systems, then, were in conflict. And it was a conflict that
began to be settled by the political resolution of the 1832 Reform Act.
Here the power of the landed interest was severely diminished by the
new franchise which granted the vote to the urban male middle class.
Government increasingly came to represent not just the towns but
those who owned property in towns and needed a growth of urban
labour. The 1834 Poor Law was one of the first demonstrations of this
urban power and created a social security system which would play a
significant role in creating the labour market that was necessary for the
urban manufacturer.

The Poor Law had two main principles and a significantly new form
of organisation. Whilst local Poor Law Unions would be responsible
for administration of the Poor Law it would be run on principles laid
down by Central Government appointed Commissioners. It was
therefore no longer possible for the local rural areas to construct
their own way of operating which would maintain their own labour
market. The nation would have a single system that would have as its
prime aim the creation of a *national* labour market. Within this market
people would move to where the work was. This would be achieved by
the two main principles of the Poor Law, that have in their way
provided some of the main themes of social security policy since then.

Firstly, the principle of less eligibility meant that anyone who
received assistance from the state would have to be less eligible – that
is, worse off – than the standard of living of the 'least independent
labourer' (Rose, 1972). In the modern world this is a simple and
straightforward notion – that someone on social security should be
worse off than the standard of living of the worst paid person in work
in the locality. Both the morality and the economics of this are clear.

Morally people must look to the labour market as their source of income – if they do not they shall be worse off than those that do. Economically this ensures that people will move onto the labour market and provide as big a pool of labour as possible. It also ensures that the labour market is the hegemonic way in which resources are distributed. Thus if the labour market decides that the wages of the least independent labourer constructed by that market is x pound, then the social security system cannot provide more than x pounds for that labourer even if he has a large number of dependents. Within the pure application of this model, need must be squeezed out of the social security system because that level is set by the wages system which has no cognisance of need.

There was a problem however. The lot of the 'least independent labourer' in Victorian urban life was truly awful. His standard of living driven by very low wage rates, appalling housing and deathly sanitation was difficult to get below. How could a standard of living be constructed which was worse than one of starvation, deprivation and early death? The innovation of the Victorians in this field has been matched by successive governments in the field of social security. Since it was not possible to provide a lower standard of living in monetary terms alone, then the social security system would move beyond the financial level to other aspects of life. From 1834 it was planned that people would receive social security if they agreed to enter and live within the workhouse. Here they would be kept alive but would lose certain human rights that others outside the workhouse would have. Given the level of civil and human rights for the labourer in mid-Victorian England was not high, the workhouse had to attack the experience of home life at its core. Entry to the workhouse would mean that the family would be split up and they would lose the right to independent living.

The 'price', therefore, of receiving social security was to enter the workhouse and here your life would be made worse than the poorest labourer outside by non-financial material and ideological changes. This innovation represents an important example of our book's overall analysis since it demonstrates that the labour market and interventions in the labour market, such as social security systems, are *not* simply concerned with money. If people could not be made to move on to the labour market by financial pressures alone, then it would be necessary to use alternative methods of pressure, involving a loss of human rights and the ideological experience of humiliation and stigma.

These two principles, that people should be worse off when on social security than when in the labour market, and that people should lose some aspects of their human rights when in receipt of social security, have run through one of our social security system's relationships with the labour market since 1834. The whole scheme was aimed at making life intolerable when in receipt of security. It succeeded.

Between the first and second world wars the Poor Law was virtually abolished but, despite local unemployment rates of above 50 per cent, life was always made worse for those on social security. Unemployment assistance and, above all, the means test made sure that if you were on security then you could not have the same rights as those who were earning wages. At any stage inspectors and assessors could enter your home and discuss with you how you spend your money. At any stage they could tell you that you had to sell a piece of furniture if they so decided. At every stage you had to prove to them that you had spent time 'genuinely seeking work'. In this way, following the principles of the Poor Law, life on the dole was made horrible. No person earning an independent living at work would have agreed to such a set of intrusions, yet for those 'living off the state', it became the norm.

We will discuss the impact of the National Insurance schemes on social security below. It is important to stress though that the post second world war social security system retained its reliance on having the right to intrude into people's lives if they were on certain forms of social security. These are called means tests. For the last 45 years, more and more people have had to experience means tests. Anyone who applies for a means tested benefit does so over a declaration which comments on their legal liability when providing wrong information. For those on what was national assistance, which then became supplementary benefit and entered the 1990s as income support, the possibility of visits by social security officers is always present. Questions can be asked about the way in which you live, which any person earning from work could refuse to answer, but if unanswered by those on income support lead to a loss of benefit. In this way the receipt of state benefit ensures that certain rights, held by all of those outside of benefit, will be lost. As we shall see below, the success of this system of withdrawing rights from those on benefit does create serious problems for governments who want to claim that they are succesful in providing those 'in need' with benefit. For one significant part of their policy is to ensure that those on means tests are placed apart from independent workers – this placing apart successfully 'puts people off' and therefore the 'take up' of benefit is limited.

THE INSURANCE PRINCIPLE

For over 150 years people have been able to insure themselves against the risk of their wages or salaries being interrupted. For those who believe in a pure market model of the labour market, this has been the preferred system of income maintenance. An insurance company works out the risk for a worker in becoming unemployed or sick. That risk then becomes the premium that the worker pays weekly to the company. When they are unemployed they receive benefit and when they are employed they pay premiums. It is in Winston Churchill's words the 'magic of averages'. Such a scheme does not need the state to intervene, and it ensures that people can 'look after themselves'.

Unfortunately this magic contains some serious flaws in its ability to carry out its spell for everyone. For under capitalism's system of distribution there is a unique and powerful flaw which goes like this: of course some people will be more likely to become unemployed than others. Those who need the 'cover' the most, that is those who are most likely to become unemployed, are those who have to pay the highest premium (since they have the highest risk – that is only fair for the insurance company). However, those who have the highest risk and therefore have the highest premium have, within a capitalist society, a tendency to have the lowest wages. For the distribution of resources through the labour market is *not* based upon risk or need but on a variety of market principles. Thus the interaction between the insurance principle and the wages system under capitalism means that those people who have to pay the highest weekly premium are paid the lowest weekly wage, whilst those people who have the lowest risk and premium are likely to be paid the higher monthly salary. The magic of averages casts no spell for the poor. A construction worker, for example, is very likely to have low wages combined with high risk. The high premiums resulting from the high risk cannot be paid on the low wage.

Consequently, for the Insurance Principle to work for many people it *must* be subsidised. This subsidy takes two forms – from employers and from the State. Again employers will be most interested in subsidising their employees' insurance with regard to labour that they value. Labour which they value is likely to be receiving decent remuneration in any case, so the employers' contribution is a perk and not such a necessity. Labour which they don't value receives low wages and therefore needs the subsidy, but is of such little value that it will not receive it. Again the magic does not work. Employers only contribute to the insurance of poorer workers if they are made to by the State.

The state also contributes. It is this way that the National Insurance Scheme was set up. This took place through two main periods of legislation – the 1911 National Insurance Act and the post-war Insurance legislation based on the Beveridge report. Both were firmly based upon a particular view of the labour market and both have had most significant effects upon the way in which labour is culturally produced in this country.

The 1911 'National' Insurance Act covered only three and three-quarter million employees for limited periods of unemployment and sickness (Gilbert, 1972). The scheme was financed by contributions from the employer, the employee and the state. For those people covered it was a breakthrough since it guaranteed those covered against applying for the Poor Law for the period that they were covered. The state and employer subsidy enabled certain sets of workers who had middling risks of unemployment and sickness to come under the protection of insurance. When they suffered unemployment or sickness these workers were covered by benefits that they received as of right and not by having to go through certain tests of rights or means. There were however several important effects upon the labour market which continued throughout the next 80 years.

Firstly, as a contribution scheme it was incomplete and in both 1911 and 1948 was very deliberately so. In fact the 1911 scheme covered only a small proportion of the population, excluded were the unskilled or semi-skilled, and part-time and seasonal workers. This exclusivity means that some elements of labour were not valued by taking a part in the scheme. The aim of the scheme was to maintain the skill base provided by one small section of the labour force. They were to be protected from the immanent effects of the labour market, protected from having to take up unskilled work for brief periods of time because of shortages of skilled work. This not only served to maintain technical skill, but also reinforced the social standing of skilled workers which would have been damaged by bouts of unemployment and eroding living standards. It, therefore, supported their specific position in the community. If this position and standard of living could be destroyed by a brief period of unemployment, then respectable working-class families would also be destroyed. Thus divisions within the labour market based upon skill were to be maintained through divisions in the social security system. The divisions which rewarded differently in work ensured that the divisions rewarded differently out of work.

Secondly, it covered the removal from the threat of the Poor Law or means tested benfits for a limited period only. If the unemployment that the worker suffered was 'frictional' and not structural then the cover was sufficient. If in 1911 it lasted for longer than 13 weeks and if, in 1990 it lasted longer than 26 weeks, then it was necessary to turn to the means tested scheme. Equally the level of benefit was set by the Insurance principle and later by Government. It was important that people should not receive benefits as of right which were higher than their level of wages. Consequently the wages level (worked out, lest we forget, on no basis of need whatsoever) had to set a ceiling for the benefit level if the wages system were to be maintained.

Thirdly, the sectionalism of its approach, designed to maintain the divisions of the labour market, firmly reproduced the gender divisions. In 1911 no women in paid work were covered by the scheme. Their labour and their skills were thought of as insufficiently important to protect them from the degradation of the Poor Law. Women working outside of the labour market in unpaid domestic labour had no cover at all for sickness or unemployment:

> women, who as wives and mothers or sisters and daughters are giving up their lives to the care of the home are not insured under the Bill. Working with others in the home is penalised by exclusion from Insurance, and a premium is put on earning money wages. Not only so, but every year which an unmarried girl devotes to 'home duties' after she leaves school is reckoned to her disadvantage. (Lawrence, 1911)

The 1911 Insurance Act enshrined the process that completely ignores all domestic labour as a part of the whole process of labour in society. The women involved and their labour was deemed of so little value that the removal of the threat of the workhouse from their lives was immaterial. This was direct discrimination between male paid labour, female paid labour and female domestic labour.

The Beveridge Report and the legislation that followed it extended the National Insurance Act to the largest number of working people ever covered. However it is essential to note that the legislation passed and implemented since then did *not* provide a national minimum standard *nor* universal benefits. And it failed to carry out both of these principles for reasons of the possible interference with the labour market.

Beveridge saw the provision of unemployment benefit as taking place in exchange for the successful meeting of certain conditions. Firstly they would have, when unemployed, to keep themselves 'fit for service', and secondly they would have to have paid contributions over the previous period in full. If both criteria were met then benefit would be paid as of right, with no recourse to the means test or the workhouse. If they failed on any account, then both Beveridge and the ensuing legislation maintained the importance of a punishing collection of means tested benefits that would be lower than the National Insurance Benefits and would provide some pain in their provision.

Rigorous application of the tests undermined attempts at a universal benefits scheme and reproduced, within the experience of those receiving benefits, the divisiveness that existed within the labour market and between the paid labour market and the unpaid domestic labour market.

Women at the time were critical of this divisiveness in the Beveridge plans

It is here that the plan falls short of really being national in character, where it shuts out or exempts from all direct participation over 9 million adult women, where it imposes a special financial burden on men alone.... The error lies in denying to married women, rich and poor, housewife or paid worker an independent personal status. From this error springs a crop of injustices, complications and difficulties, personal marital and administrative, involving in the long run men both married and unmarried and the unmarried as well as the married women. (Abbot and Bompas, 1943)

We must stress again that their exclusion from the National Insurance Benefits ensured that women who were in need had either to rely totally on their male partners' contribution record and a share in that benefit, or if they had become separated had to rely on the means tested benefits that the National Insurance Scheme was meant to be removing them from.

Further, Beveridge and the post-war Government's commitment to a certain form of labour market, which stressed full-time and permanent employment, meant that only those persons in regular organised labour for nearly every week of the year could gain unemployment benefit. Casual employment, irregular employment and part-time employment could provide insufficient contributions to entitle the worker to insurance benefits.

Thus a system which was labelled as 'universal' was only universal for a particular form of male dominated employment pattern. In this way the priviliged form of social security system was designed to reinforce one kind of labour market and to punish another for whom the means tests remained.

CONTEMPORARY LABOUR MARKETS AND SOCIAL SECURITY SYSTEM

Both of the country's social security systems, then, have direct relationships to a form of labour market. They are intended to create and recreate a particular social relationship to that labour market.

Means tests are meant to ensure that people are frightened of being made unemployed and do not 'rest' in that state when they become unemployed. The contribution principle is tied to those who are in full-time permanent, regular work and provides certain benefits to those people who are in such work. These benefits will only come to those that are committed to this style of work. If you 'voluntarily' give up that work then you receive no unemployment benefit for half a year.

The first is a powerful stick to reinforce people's relationship to a certain kind of work, and the second is a possible carrot for those who are engaged in that form of work and a stick to those who are not.

We believe that the historical and contemporary argument which demonstrates the state role in constructing such a labour market is unanswerable (Kincaid, 1968). The point of this chapter though, is to look at the repercussions of this social security system on the nature of the labour market in the late 1980s and early 1990s.

Firstly, and of great significance, all of the methods that have been evolved over time to demonstrate the horribleness of being unemployed on state benefits actually works for most people. In short, everything from the workhouse test, the means test, the genuinely seeking work test and the back up editorials in the gutter press attacking those people on unemployment benefit has worked and entered the culture of working people.

Under these circumstances workers are so frightened that they may lose the jobs that they hang onto them tenaciously. The effect of this, probably more than any other Government policy, has been to increase the immobility of labour and the resistance to enforced mobility caused by unemployment. This powerful and ingrained cultural fear of becoming unemployed, reinforced by the present Government's continual changes in social security policy aimed at making life on the dole more horrible, has ensured that the restructuring of the economy which has been the hallmark of post-war European economies has been much more difficult in Britain.

A social security system which punishes unemployment will contradict an economic policy which needs both frictional and structural unemployment. With such a system, employed people will struggle hard to avoid becoming unemployed, With such a social security system, people once unemployed will struggle hard to re-enter the labour market, perhaps at any level of skill. Thus even a short spell of unemployment could mean that the worker takes a less skilled job simply in order to stop being unemployed. Whilst ministers may say that becoming unemployed is a necessary part of changes in the labour market and should be welcomed by workers, the workers will not see unemployment as anything other than humiliation and being moved 'beyond the pale' of society.

When faced with unemployment, workers will fight it; when faced with a change that may or may not lead to it, workers will fight it; when faced with any change in their work practices at all, workers will judge such a change against their fear of unemployment; when faced with a new technology or a new machine it will be judged against the possibility of it making the person unemployed. Under these circumstances it is no use the Secretary of State for Employment arguing for the acceptance of change and periods of unemployment; for the Secretary of State for Social Security is persuading people that life on the dole is extremely unpleasant and shameful. The success of this social security policy has ensured continual defence against change by the British workforce, and therefore much greater difficulty in restructuring the economy.

In the long term, by placing those who are unemployed beyond the orthodox sets of relationships enjoyed by the rest of the population, by creating this 'world apart', they have also succeeded in making long term unemployed people feel separate in that 'world apart'. For if in the short term it proved impossible for all of the people to re-enter the labour market, if in fact there were no jobs to re-enter, then all of those humiliations and pressures could not actually work. They would have to be suffered with no recourse to the possibility of work.

It is under these circumstances, caught between pressure to get work and the non-existence of work, that the long term unemployed person feels that the labour market (both when economically active and when economically inactive) is simply *not* for them. By withdrawing completely to the world of unemployment, a world placed by policy beyond other sets of social relationships, re-entry then becomes a problem. Ironically, this problem of re-entry has been created by the social security and labour market policies that were meant to solve it.

Another problem caused by the success of the means test in making benefits unattractive, has been the Conservative Government's attempts to ensure that means tested benefits become the main way in which social security is 'targetted' to the individuals in need. Family Credit is paid to workers who are in low-wage jobs and have certain sizes of families. People can claim the benefit, which acts as a sort of top-up on wages. However the benefit is only granted if the claimant undergoes a means test and the experience of such tests has become so successfully punishing that people will not apply for them. Thus the Government's policy of 'targetting' such resources means that in 1989 less than 60 per cent of the people who were eligible for Family Credit actually received it (Low Pay Unit, 1989). Again this was a result of the success of the means test.

A further contradiction wrought by the large number of means tested benefits available to people on low income is the poverty trap. One of the successes of the Conservative Government's economic policy has been to increase the incentive to high salary earners by reducing the marginal tax rate to 40 per cent. This reduction was meant to ensure that such people would have incentives to work harder for the extra pound. However the poverty trap created by mean tested benefits has created a marginal loss of benefit rate of over 80 per cent for many people on poor pay. For them, an extra 40 pounds per week earned through an extra 10 hours overtime would only provide 8 pounds. Such a marginal rate of return for labour has ensured that, for the poorest, the means tested social security system acts as a direct disincentive to work longer hours. The National Insurance system had been created to reward a certain form of labour – regular, permanent and full-time. Again, as with the means test, this combined social security and labour market policy has been successful. Certain sorts of paid labour is rewarded and is hung on to. Yet as all the statistics of changes in the labour market show, it is this form of labour which is in decline. The Conservative Governments' employment White Papers of 1984 and 1988 both heralded the growth of part-time, temporary and irregular forms of work as the growth area of the labour market. Yet workers who move into those groups are almost certain to find their national insurance contribution record inadequate for the receipt of benefit. Such work, when interrupted, leaves the worker at the mercy of the means tested benefits of income support.

We have then two different systems of state income support that
have been created to reinforce a certain kind of labour discipline. Both
have been successful, yet are playing a significant part in rewarding
those people who struggle to stay in precisely those forms of labour
that the Government's Employment Department is encouraging them
to move out of! Social security policies created for the Victorian and
post second world war labour markets are of no use to the labour
market of the 1990s, except as a distinct hindrance to skill and labour
development.

6 The Reform of the Unions

If employers and the state have undervalued labour, at least trade unions have tried to oppose this process. They have done this through the traditional methods of collective bargaining and political lobbying and agitation. In recent years these efforts have continued, but in the face of three major challenges to the trade union movment. Firstly, the state has passed laws which have been put forward as reforming the unions, but which were aimed principally at weakening the movement's ability to use strikes and other actions to achieve wage advances and other economic objectives, but also at increasing the individual rights of trade unionists with respect to union discipline. Secondly, mass unemployment, which produced a major drop in membership, compelled the movement to contemplate reforming itself, and led to anxious internal debates about the direction of reform (the 'new realism' debate). Thirdly, the trade union movement, in the 1970s as well as in the 1980s, found itself challenged by sections of its own membership as being based on sectarianism – this charge was made especially by women and ethnic minorities.

That the trade union movement should have found itself faced by these challenges was obviously the result of the political and economic circumstances of recent years. But it was also a result of the history of the union movement which had made it what it was. In the 1980s it was still very heavily dominated by an economic outlook, centralised administration, sectarianism, and a responsiveness to the activists rather than to the broad mass of members.

To understand something of the events of recent years, therefore, an appreciation of trade unionism's history in Britain is needed.

TRADE UNIONS AND HISTORY

It took the trade union movment at least a century of experiment in order to begin to organise across a range of skills in the labour market on a national scale. Trade unionists in the early nineteenth century struggled to achieve 'combination' (collective organisation) and then to find forms within which workers could defend their working conditions and give expression to their embryonic political demands. Such struggle ranged from Luddism (Hobsbawm, 1964) to early, shortlived general unions and the more modest, but enduring, local trade societies of skilled workers. This early phase of development was taken up with the problem of organising and bargaining in conditions of illegality, owing to the Combination Acts, as well as with grandiose attempts to organise across trades and skills in tandem with the small scale, local organisation of craft workers. It was a phase of development in which the union movement was searching for legality and political identity, together with social acceptance.

The second phase of development around the 'new model unions' dates from the mid nineteenth century and here we see the the achievement of viable, national organisations for groups of skilled workers. These organisations – the Amalgamated Society of Engineers (established in 1851) and its imitators – were conservative and sectionalist unions, based on a cautious but stable organisation rather than a liberating and mobilising class identity and politics. The 'new model unions' represented the class fraction within which they organised, but they eschewed any wider class practice until, perhaps, the end of the century.

They have of course been the object of political criticism as a result of this; they have been condemned as constructing a 'labour aristocracy'. This criticism is somewhat one-sided. Craft unions certainly fought to value and revalue their members, and in a free labour market this could, and did, widen differentials between themselves and the mass of other unorganised workers. And it also widened the ideological, political and social differences within the working class.

But we must not undervalue their contribution to working class culture in organisational and political terms. Firstly, the new model unions provided favourable conditions for the organisational development of the working classes through the foundation of the Trades Union Congress (TUC), the union movement's central organisation, which began in the year 1868. The movement realised through this national Congress and organisation for all trade unions the possibility of becoming a truly *national* movement. Secondly, in this period the skilled workers began to participate in parliamentary democracy. Presumably national organisation meant much greater potential mobilisation and use of skilled working class power and resources. It also constructed a fraction of the working class as a new and viable political constituency for both the Tories and, more particularly, the Liberals. Consequently, it enabled skilled workers to enter the national political arena.

So whilst the skilled worker was sectionalist, sexist and in some senses an exploiter of the less skilled, he nevertheless moved union organisation on, away from the pre-capitalist mode of organisation of working people. And for a small fraction of the working class to achieve national organisation and status was a fundamental organisational breakthrough for the working-class as a whole. The legal and political conditions prevailing in the mid-nineteenth century were not readily conducive to such an outcome and as such it stands as a remarkable achievement in working class history.

Moreover, once established as a movement of national significance, the union movement provided conditions in which more progressive political ideas could also be developed. Many skilled workers supported the Tory and Liberal parties, but amongst some workers there was emerging an interest in a political party for the working-class. The Social-Democratic Federation and the Independent Labour Party both developed in the later years of the century and established some support amongst the working class.

The 'New Unionism' of the 1880s, which was inspired by the match-girls, who went on strike successfully in 1888, and the rapid unionisation of London gas-workers and dockers, was a response by less skilled workers to the process of commodification, characterised by poverty-level wages, long hours, dangerous conditions, sporadic employment and autocratic management. Such super-exploitation led to the gradual organisation of such workers in trade unions that were organisationally and politically more open and militant than the unions of the craftsmen. They were helped by a variety of political organisations (the Fabians, the Social Democratic Federation and the Independent Labour Party), militants from craft unions (Burns and Mann) and home-grown leaders (Thorne and Tillett). Trade unionism had made a start on organising across a wider spectrum of the working class, achieving a union density of about 12 per cent by 1901 (Jackson, 1988).

The process of constructing counter-hegemonic politics was under-way with the setting up of the Labour Representation Committee (LRC) in 1900. This body demonstrated the strategic importance of the TUC to the labour movement at the turn of the century; for the LRC was an outgrowth of the TUC's Parliamentary Committee. It was the only politically viable organisation that could successfully unite representatives of the old and the new unionism and the various socialist societies at the time. Political 'take-off' was, however, the result of the class reaction of capital to organised labour; the famous Taff Vale case in 1901, in which the Law Lords decided that unions could be sued for damages caused by their officers, signalled to the trade union movement that industrial action alone was not enough. Affiliations to the LRC more than doubled in the next two years and a union fund was raised to support Labour MPs.

The historical evidence points to the progressive organisational and political attempts by the labour movement to protect and reproduce the value of labour. Capital was commodifying labour and trying to do so in a way that radically devalued it – it sought to cheapen and deskill labour, to organise production in dehumanised conditions, to use labour with disregard for its health and safety, and generally to reduce labour to a ruinous state. The unions resisted this devaluation of labour – they struggled to improve wages and conditions and challenged capital's authority both at the workplace and in Parliament.

The history of the movement's organisation demonstrates how it began as a narrowly sectionalist economic movement – with a concern to improve wages and conditions of particular stratas of workers – and began to grow into a more widely based and political one. Its political development, it is clear, grew out of its need to defend the general interests of working people by countering the attacks on the union movement's organisation.

One hundred years after the onset of new unionism, the British trade union movement was still developing and changing. We will see below that in the 1980s it was being forcibly reformed by the state, but, more importantly, it was reconstituting itself in order to appeal more effectively to unorganised sections of the working class and to sections of its own membership which had been ignored.

LEGAL REFORMS IN THE 1980S

In the 1980s the state carried through a radical programme of legal reform of the trade unions. Four Acts made up the package of 'step by step' reform: the Employment Acts of 1980, 1982 and 1988 and the Trade Union Act of 1984.

The Employment Act of 1980 was the Thatcher Government's first major step in its legal reform of the unions. It was explained as being reform designed to achieve a restoration of the 'balance' in industrial relations. It dealt with secret ballots on strikes and other union decisions, picketing, secondary action, the closed shop and various other matters. It was said to be concerned also with protecting individuals in relation to the actions of trade unions.

The chief legal changes produced by the whole programme of reform included narrowed immunities for industrial action, ending of legal secondary picketing, changes in the law regarding union membership, requirements for ballots on elections and other matters, and the introduction of a Commissioner for the rights of trade union members.

Government statements in the 1980s suggested a duality of motives. There was much talk of shifting the balance back towards the individual and the need to make unions more democratic, but the general concern of the Thatcher administration seemed to be to create more labour market flexibility, which was seen as obstructed by industrial relations institutions. Thus, it appeared, there was a desire to cut down the unions' ability to influence pay (which the Government saw as directly linked to the number of jobs) and an emphasis on empowering the individual within the union (which was described as promoting union democracy).

Whilst the trade unions were complaining loudly that the Government were out to neuter the movement and that the criticisms of them as abusing their power and being undemocratic were false, public opinion seemed to accept some of the negative views on unions. Public opinion polls in late 1983, for instance, found a majority of people believing that trade unions had too much power in Britain. They were also against secondary industrial action by trade unionists and the closed shop. On the other hand, an overwhelming majority of people still considered that trade unions were essential to protect workers' interests (MORI, 1983).

What did the public want? Perhaps it wanted the unions to find a new style and content of action – one which was more reasonable. It was difficult for the union movement to see it in this way. It was hard to accept that there could be popular sympathy with the Thatcher Government's reforms, which were so transparently a ruling class attack on one of the most powerful organisations of the working class. Some people undoubtedly felt that Government propaganda had temporarily confused British people.

These were difficult times for union leaders to be self-critical. The mass unemployment had caused a serious loss of membership. There was also a political collapse with which to contend: the Labour Party's support amongst trade unionists fell from over 50 per cent in the 1979 general election to 39 per cent in June 1983 (MORI, 1983). How many union leaders had the composure to see all this happening and still find the confidence to embark on a critical examination of union organisation and strategy?

The Thatcher administration represented itself as making the unions more democratic, strengthening the individual rights of the member against the union, and restoring the balance of power. The tacit linkage of these reforms with the Government's attacks on 'excessive' pay settlements negotiated by the unions and inflexible labour markets also continued.

The trade union movement capaigned against the legislation and even tried to prohibit the acceptance of public funds under the Employment Act scheme. But effective resistance to the legal reforms proved difficult and trade unions found themselves legally handicapped in particular disputes by the new laws. One notorious dispute which took place at the News International plant in London's East End showed how the new laws could be exploited by hard-nosed employers.

At the end of the 1980s the International Labour Organisation (ILO), a part of the United Nations, criticised various aspects of the new legal framework, including the ban on sympathy action, restrictions on the unions' rights to discipline members, the ability of employers to limit legal industrial action by splitting companies artificially, and the ability of employers to dismiss strikers. The implication was that trade union rights had been undermined by the Government. Accusations of union-bashing, however, cut little ice with the British Government.

The Government's Trade Union Act, which required unions to ballot their members on political funds, did however lead to a major success for the union movement in what was often experienced as a period of great adversity. Union after union secured large majorities in favour of retaining or even introducing new political funds. Some of the well known public sector unions were amongst those voting to set up a political fund, including the Institution of Professional Civil Servants and NALGO. The unions felt that this was an instance where they had gone out and campaigned to the membership on the need for political influence and where the result had been overwhemingly, and unambiguously positive.

This particular episode demonstrated that, although the legal restrictions of the 1980s made it difficult for the unions to win their battles with capital or the state, they did not make hegemonic practice impossible.

UNEMPLOYMENT AND RENEWAL

The biggest pressure on the trade unions to embark on reform came from the effects of mass unemployment. The TUC, in a consultative paper in 1984, called *TUC Strategy*, made it clear that it was concerned not only at the way the Government had been attempting to limit the role of unions and shut them out of national decisions, but also at the loss of membership and the difficulties the unions would face in recruiting new members.

The concern was more than justified. Unemployment stood at three million in 1984 and only fell below two million in 1989. These are the official figures, which have attracted much comment because of frequent, and politically motivated, revision in the methods of compilation by the Government – some experts have attempted to provide alternative estimates which suggest much higher levels of unemployment. But whatever the precise figures, unemployment had drastic and immediate effects on trade unions, although, as the table below shows, some unions suffered much more than others.

Table 3   Membership of selected TUC unions

Union	1979	1988	% change
TGWU	2 086 281	1 312 853	−37
AEU	1 298 580	793 610	−39
GMB	967 153	864 021	−11
NALGO	753 226	754 701	0
MSF[1]	(691 954)	653 000	− 6
NUPE	691 770	635 070	− 8
USDAW	470 017	396 724	−16
EETPU[2]	420 000	329 914 (1987)	−21

Source: TUC

Notes: [1]The Manufacturing, Science and Finance union (MSF) resulted from the merger of ASTMS and TASS.
[2]The EETPU was expelled from the TUC.

The largest unions experienced the largest losses, whilst public service unions such as NALGO and NUPE more or less held up their membership.

The 1980s saw a decline in production industries and a growth in service occupations: a shift which was hardly favourable to union fortunes given the movement's strength in the former and weakness in the latter.

The trends towards hi-tech industries, the shift from public to private sector employment, the growth of small businesses, and regional redistribution of economic activity were all being nervously watched by the union movement. The growth of white collar work, the increasing share of women in paid employment, and the growth of part-time, temporary and self-employment were all interpreted as adverse developments from the point of view of union membership.

The 1984 strategy review conducted by the TUC was part of the process of managing the process of union change. Various initiatives followed. The trade unions saw the need to step up recruitment activities and by the late 1980s union officers were spending more time dealing with recruitment and organisation (*TUC Bulletin*, November 1989, No.37). Much of this recruitment effort was targetted by union reports on part-time, mainly women, workers within the private services. As we shall see in the next section, the unions also gave more thought to how they actually represented women.

THE UNIONS AND EQUAL RIGHTS

A hegemonic trade union practice must attempt to mobilise all members and supporters. Merely possessing a constitution that suggests a strong commitment to socialism and democracy without distinction is not a guarantee of unity and solidarity. In fact it may act as a substitute for unity. Trade union and Labour Party constitutions can be, and are, used mythically so that their mere possession are deemed to denote democracy and socialism. However in the 1970s and 80s what has been connoted is often sexism and racism. Both are, of course, outlawed by the various constitutions.

The issue of sexism in the unions began to be confronted in the 1970s. For example, the struggle for the acceptance of the Woman's Charter took place in different union bodies and culminated in the TUC issuing a Charter, *Equality for Women within Trade Unions*, in 1979. This meant that the affiliated unions were formally accepting that unions were failing to provide full democracy for women members.

As a result of the work done on equality in the 1970s, the unions in the 1980s were becoming increasingly aware of the need to be more relevant to women and ethnic minorities. The critique of the unions as too concerned with white males became more and more biting.

The 1979 TUC Charter on women's equality within trade unions called on individual unions to take various steps: these included declaring a commitment to involving women at all levels of the union, examining the structure of the union, providing additional seats or co-option to decision-making bodies where necessary, setting up advisory bodies, and making various other provisions and arrangements which would aid equality. It was not a mandatory programme, and progress has been slow. A survey carried out by the South East Region TUC Women's Committee in 1988 found that unions have introduced a variety of measures to encourage women's participation: women's or equality committees, women's officers and reserved seats on executive committees were very common. Nevertheless their survey revealed, 'In almost all cases, women are less well represented at conference and on the executive than in the union overall' (SERTUC, 1989).

Trade unions were organising more women in 1990 than in 1979. Women in public sector unions are more valued than they are in private sector unions, and have made more advances, particularly in regard to pay, recruitment and promotion (Laffin, 1989). However, overall we still do not have equal pay (despite the legislation) and the problem with job segregation is still a major source of discrimination. Although unions cannot solve external problems – such as the domestic division of labour – they could do much more to mitigate their effects by bargaining more strongly on child care policies and issues both for parents in general, and women in particular.

As we have already indicated (see Chapter 3), racial discrimination is a fundamental problem in Britain. Whilst capital undervalues and devalues labour in general, the situation of black workers is aggravated by the widespread presence of 'race thinking' and practice in our society. Such thinking and practice has also characterised the trade union movement despite its formal atttachment to equal opportunities, and despite years of denying the existence of racism among trade unionists. For many years prior to the 1970s, it had tended to see racial problems as a function of 'the unwillingness of black immigrants to "integrate", thus transferring the onus for action to black workers' (Miles and Phizacklea, 1981, p.246). Unions simply failed to take an active interest in issues of race and anti-discrimination – even when they had large black memberships.

Complacency gave way to a new awareness and a new policy direction in the 1970s. Under the impact of a number of disputes, internal and external criticism, the trade union movement began to sit up and take notice of race relations. As Miles and Phizacklea have emphasised, a number of disputes involving black workers who alleged discrimination by white trade union members and officials contradicted the view that racism was not a problem. Key disputes occurred at Mansfield Hosiery Mills Ltd in 1972, and at Imperial Typewriters Ltd, Leicester. According to Miles and Phizacklea, 'these two disputes clearly showed that trade unionists and trade union officials could be guilty of discriminatory practice' (1981, p.256).

There had in addition been a growing concern inside the trade union movement about racial discrimination in Britain. This surfaced in local trade union conferences and locally based union committees in the Midlands and the North aimed at combating discrimination and changing union policy. There was also support from some full-time trade union officials who were aware of the weakness of the TUC position and were working to develop a more positive policy.

A third factor in the situation was the National Front's participation in the general elections of 1974. Whilst making little progress politically, the National Front made their mark through the media and through street demonstrations which were often violent. Paradoxically, its development provided a clear enemy for union leaders and in some sense made it easier to attack racism within the movement.

More pressure for change came from a Select Committee on Race Relations, which reported in 1974 and included some criticism of the TUC (and the CBI) for failing to take adequate steps to tackle racial discrimination. The organisational response of the TUC was to shift responsibility for race relations from the International Committee to the Organisational and Industrial Relations Department, thereby placing it in in the mainstream of TUC work. It also appointed an Equal Rights Committee as a sub-committee of the General Council.

Strangely, discrimination appears not to have lessened the attachment of black people to trade unions; both black women and men are more likely to join unions than their white counterparts. A study by the Policy Studies Institute showed that in the early 1980s 56 per cent of black employees were union members as against only 47 per cent of white employees. Black members, however, were much less likely to hold an elected post in their unions (Brown, 1984).

These findings do need to be treated with some caution. It may be that other factors obscure the effect of discrimination on union membership. Brown (1984), for example, argues that the greater propensity of black workers to join unions is largely a feature of the jobs they do. If he is correct on this point, and his comparisons of union membership data according to job level categories suggests he is, then the unions may still be deterring potential members by their racism.

The union movement was still taking initiatives on equality in the late 1980s. In 1988 the TUC set up a new Equal Rights Department. This followed a Congress decision to do more on women's issues and race relations. Further initiatives followed in 1989 when the TUC set up a special panel to develop a union equal pay strategy, and organised a TUC Women's Action Day in March. At the 1989 Congress the TUC agreed to increase the number of seats reserved for women on the General Council (the TUC's executive body). Also in that year, it organised seminars to help unions tackle racial equality. Clearly, the TUC policy on discrimination since the 1970s heralds a significant change; it is now concerned with combating sex and racial discrimination and the growth of neofascism. It campaigns against them vigorously – along with the Labour Party.

In summing up this section, we would say, that it would seem that the trade union movement of the 1950s and 60s did not take sex discrimination seriously and its policy on race was complacent and mistaken. In the 1980s the unions have persisted in their attempts to reform themselves, confronting a difficult policy debate over the rightness of positive action, as opposed to a merely formal constitutional equality. In these attempts to move towards more equality, they have struggled to free themselves of the 'integrationism' policy on racism – partly as a result of the politics of the left wing of the movement and partly as a result of the defensive and courageous practice of black trade unionists. It was increasingly realised that whilst racism devalued black workers, so did 'integration'. Anti-racism and equal opportunity education played a part in combating such negativity but it is a long and continuing struggle. This is partly due to the fact that racist devaluation is even more marked amongst employers.

BUSINESS UNIONISM

Trade unions have a long history of being told that they are now no longer needed, that they are in danger of becoming extinct, or that they are 'dinosaurs' or anachronistic. The truth is that the trade unions are part and parcel of the flow of social and historical development and continually move between constructing the future and trying to get up to date. In other words, there never will be a time in capitalist society when unions will not be making and remaking themselves; nor will there ever be a time when someone is not advising them to change before it is too late.

Accordingly the recent warning to the trade union movement in the White Paper, *Employment for the 1990s*, may be recognised as just one of the latest of a long line of warnings to the unions:

> Over the period since 1979, the number of trade union members has been falling, from over 13.2 million to just under 10.6 million. Many of the sectors of employment where trade union membership has traditionally been concentrated, such as manufacturing and public sector industries, have declined. The growing service industries are unlikely to provide trade unions with recruitment on the same scale. Trade unions will attract and retain members only if they come to terms with economic realities and if they adapt themselves to the changing needs of their members in the 1990s. (Employment Department, 1988, p.17)

Of course the Government was right that these economic changes and the changing needs of members present important challenges. Unions have to make their history under the conditions which prevail and there is nothing which guarantees that they will spontaneously and rapidly make correct adjustments – after all, history is full of mistakes and accidents.

The Government, in its 1988 White Paper, made quite clear the specific union reforms it wanted to see. Firstly, it wanted the unions to be less militant as organisations; they were to recognise that the members' interests were not served by conflict. Secondly, it wanted the unions to shift from defending workers by regulating working practices ('defending out-of-date methods of working') to being more concerned about pensions and training. Thirdly, it wanted unions to shift on bargaining objectives: pay should, in the Government's opinion, be linked to company performance and local labour market conditions. Presumably this would mean unions moving away from setting objectives on the basis of seeking improvements in the standard of living of members (which tend thus to be geared to the national inflation rate) or on the basis of the national 'going rate'. Fourthly, it wanted the unions to 'see' that efficiency, profitability and flexibility in working practices were the best guarantee of jobs. Finally, it wanted the unions to come to terms with the fact that union recognition by many employers would only be on the basis of single-union and no-strike agreements. This aspect of the Government vision is slightly puzzling: was it saying that union recognition for bargaining purposes was itself non-negotiable? Was it saying that the unions should accept the unilateral determination of the terms of recognition by the employer? Or, was it really stating an empirical fact that some employers were so recalcitrant and unitarist in their mentality that they were not prepared to accept union recognition on any but the stated terms?

THE UNIONS AND MOVING ON

Government visions of the ideal trade union movement are one thing, actuality is another. A handful of 'new realists' and business unions may aspire to the model of trade unionism extolled by the Government, but the majority of trade unionists do not.

The restrictive law of the 1980s has not defeated the unions. Since the Miners' debacle in 1984–5, unions have begun to elaborate alternative forms of industrial action. Whilst the numbers of strikes decreased with rising unemployment and under the Thatcher Governments, there has been a series of large-scale stoppages since 1978. These have been undertaken by workers in a wide range of industries and services: the engineers (1979), public service and ancillary workers (1979), the national steel strike (1980), civil servants (1981), National Health Service staff, railway workers, electricity, gas and water (1982), miners (1984–5), teachers (1985–6), national newspaper workers (1986), and seamen (1988).

In 1989 industrial relations commentators began to identify a new mood of militancy in the trade union movement. There were again major disputes; these involved the railway workers and, in the National Health Service, the ambulance staff. The attack on the public sector by the Government's economic and social programmes stoked up many grievances amongst public sector workers in the 1980s. The two big disputes of 1989 both reflected a mood in which such workers were fed up with being treated with callous indifference because they were public sector workers; and both also showed that workers were no longer prepared to accept the devaluing of their work by their employers and, ultimately, the Government itself.

What was also interesting about the rail and ambulance disputes in 1989 was the key role played by the media and public opinion. The unions concerned, chiefly the NUR and NUPE, managed to orchestrate their industrial action in such a way as to maintain, and develop, public support – even though there was a hostile Government, judiciary and media. Public support was so clear cut that the media had to reflect it. That support was not a simplistic, spontaneous gift but a carefully honed product of hegemonic leadership and discipline.

People have continued to watch the trade union movement over the last ten years – watching for signs of change, atrophy, new growth, anything in fact which will provide a pointer to the future significance of the movment in British society (Coates and Topham, 1988; Kelly, 1988; McIlroy, 1988). Some stress its experience as one of continuity; they emphasise that it continues to be a large and voluntary organisation of working people playing a vital role in the pursuit of democracy and justice. Other people emphasise how well the unions weathered the storms of the 1980s: membership had held up better than might have been expected, the numbers of shop stewards and lay officials are impressive, unions are financially sound, and the wage gains of their members have been the despair of the Thatcher Government. Even more positively, the unions came through the trap set by the Government over political fund ballots with flying colours, they have switched resources to membership recruitment, and recruitment drives in the 1990s could well re-launch the movement on its long-term trend towards organising a larger proportion of workers (a trend evident over the last 100 years).

Nevertheless the 1980s were a turning point for trade unions and it will be a movement of a different character which will have to confront the inherent problems of managing sectionalism and of managing the relationship between economic and political endeavours.

Defining the essence of this difference in character is not easy and is certainly not to be simply pinned down to specific organisational changes. There is no doubt however that the hard work of trade union leaders, activists and members, which was produced in response to the legal changes, the unemployment and economic shifts, and the demand for equality within the unions, has led to a very different experience of being in a trade union. This difference of experience probably comes down to a new quality in the internal relations of the union. The leadership has learned to listen to, and value, the wishes of the membership more than it used to. This is partly shown by the new appreciation of the need to be representative of the membership –

really and not just formally – which has been learnt more deeply than before. The need to value what members do as workers has been learnt to some extent. This was true generally as the movement began to campaign for a high skill and high pay workforce in an increasingly competitive world. It was learnt especially in the public services – it had to be as a practical necessity because industrial action in the public services had to value the service to consumers as much as it valued the wage rises that it hoped to win if public support was to be maintained. And the need to value all union members, women as well as men, blacks as well as whites, was learnt.

Of course the unions do not emerge from the 1980s completely reformed and now perfect, but they have moved nearer towards what they should be – democratic organisations for all working people which are capable of acting as one of the most important of the instruments for the effective organisation of their lives.

In our view, the next few years for the trade unions will be ones in which the movement's relationship with Europe and with the Labour Party will be very important.

Looking to Europe, British trade unions and the TUC have belatedly seen opportunities for their members in the single European market and the social charter. The latter promises to provide a raft of trade union and workplace rights that have been undermined by rampant Thatcherism. The social charter was proposed by the European Commission to accompany the move towards a single European market in 1992. It set out a set of European rights on living and working conditions, fair pay, social protection, freedom of association, a right to collective bargaining, rights to vocational training, equality for women and men, provision for disabled people, workers' rights to information, consultation and participation, and various other rights and provision. In a vote on the charter in the European Council only Britain voted against adopting a statement on it. Precisely what will be saved of the original charter will depend on the negotiations which will inevitably surround its further progress and the effectiveness of the Thatcher Government's opposition. Of course, should the Labour Party win the next general election, the charter will no doubt be adopted.

The trade union movement's relationship with the Labour Party has been undergoing re-evaluation and it is still not clear how this will evolve in the next couple of years. However, the end of the bloc vote, closed shops and pre-emptive strikes (especially in the public sector) are on the cards. In return, trade unions will increasingly look to new forms of valuing labour such as rights to information, industrial democracy, a shorter working week, substantial training and retraining programmes and serious childcare programmes. The Labour Party itself will need to look to elaborating a serious process of democratic accountability and political education. If we enter the 21st century with the current profile of political literacy, the labour movement will make slow and uncertain progress.

OLD LANDMARKS AND NEW TIMES

Earlier we talked about the unions and a collective concern to improve wages and conditions and challenge capital's authority. This concern and challenge is not a neat, unitary practice. It has been, and is, extremely contradictory in the sense that trade union practice has exhibited tendencies to incorporation both in terms of relations with employers and the state, and tendencies to pre-emptive class struggle.

Incorporation has been demonstrated by a cautious attachment to collective bargaining structures and practices, including conciliation and arbitration and joint consultation on state committees (for example NEDC). This normative process has been interrupted by bouts of pre-emptive militancy which have been largely sectionalist and occasionally hegemonic. Militant trade unionism has rarely been able to attract cross-class support or even support across a fraction within the working class. Some people argue that the latter was achieved in the General Strike of 1926, by the miners in the 1970s, and by the railway workers and the ambulance workers in 1989. The latter two have demonstrated that, with hegemonic leadership and discipline, even cross-class support is a possibility. To the extent that unions fail to mobilise class support, they fail to realise the full value of labour.

7 The Cultural Revolution in Production

INTRODUCTION

In the 1970s and 80s, whilst social democracy was succumbing (in Britain) to the New Right's laissez-faire ideology and political practice, the economic system appeared equally to be undergoing radical and rapid change. Much, but not all, of the economic change was involved with technological changes. Thus, in the late 1970s and throughout the 1980s, management in private manufacturing plants and nationalised industries introduced microelectronics into production processes, affecting the work of many manual workers. Computerisation of previously 'manual' systems and the introduction of word processors on a massive scale likewise reshaped the work of many non-manual workers during the 1980s (Daniel, 1987). This applied to all areas of the economy, including services such as banking, high street retailing by multiple stores, and the operations of civil servants working for central government.

In addition to technological change, there were attempts to reorganise production processes in manufacturing, bringing in systems based on group technology or group working. And an influx of new Japanese firms, which set up manufacturing plants, focused attention on flexible working – 'functional flexibility' – and 'just in time' systems with suppliers. Contemporary writing on these developments have coined concepts such as 'Post-Fordism', 'flexible specialisation', and 'Japanisation' in a bid to understand the emerging reality.

Before we proceed any further, we must make it clear that we do not see the developments which were taking place throughout the 1980s as simply wholesale *displacements* of what was there before. Mainly the changes were remaking and modifying the social relations and social ideas of the 1960s. Although it is also true that some of the new Japanese firms did in a sense try to make a fresh cultural start when they restricted their recruitment to young people with no previous experience of industry, or heavily screened new recruits. On the whole, however, the developments of the 1980s were attempts to overcome the central contradiction of mass production, which was the opposition

105

between a system of production which reduced the humanity of the worker to a minimum and the union resistance to this treatment.

The purpose of this chapter is therefore to lay out the nature of mass production, its inevitable social crisis in terms of trade union resistance, and its passage into 'Post-Fordist' production, a system which is still to be correctly described in the literature. We will be emphasising the social aspect over the economic in understanding this particular transition.

THE AGE OF MASS PRODUCTION

The age of mass production began in Britain during the 1920s. Of course at no time has industry been organised solely under the system of mass production, nor are we saying that mass production has suddenly ceased to exist. Rather, mass production became the leading edge of the development of productive forces, reducing the unit costs of products down to levels which made them marketable on a mass basis.

Mass production was not just an isolated development. Its beginning occurred between the two world wars, a period which saw the rise of industrial joint-stock companies, the growth in the mean size of industrial plants, and the growing concentration of output in relatively few plants in various manufacturing industries, especially the newer ones (Aldcroft, 1983). Motor car manufacturing stands out amongst the industries which were based on the system of mass production. By the mid 1930s it had already achieved substantial concentration and the largest plants were indeed already very large.

The nature of social relations in industry were profoundly changed by the arrival of mass production. For a start the nature of management–employee relations changed: the newer, larger mass production factories could not be managed in the same way that the older and smaller one-man businesses and family firms were managed. Mass production brought more remote, professional management. It also brought a new division of labour within the workforce. And it created new gender relations; for many of the newer factory workers were women.

In the motor industry, the development of the mass production system in the 1920s and 30s meant that production by semi-skilled operators replaced that by skilled tradesmen. 'And the rate of change was such that even the early cars produced for the mass market were made almost entirely by semi-skilled labour' (Turner et al., 1967, p.192).

The skilled men were employed instead on maintenance, repair, and on special work such as prototype-making.

The new factories were built in the South and the Midlands, well away from the traditional industries. The siting of new factories created new centres of population as workers were attracted to the area. For example the massive set of works at Dagenham in Essex built by the Ford Motor Company, were matched by large new housing estates which were the homes of thousands of Ford employees and their families. Masses of labour were produced on the door steps of the new factories.

FORDISM AND CONSUMPTION: THE AFFLUENT WORKERS

The workers in Fordist factories have generally been portrayed as estranged from the content of labour activity. Goldthorpe and his co-researchers, who studied car workers and other manual workers in Luton during the 1960s, connected this estrangement to consumption goals outside of work:

the meaning they gave to the activities and relationships of work was a predominantly instrumental one; work was defined and experienced essentially as a means to the pursuit of ends outside of work and usually ones relating to standards of domestic living. (Goldthorpe et al., 1969, p.164).

The newer workers in the mass production factories were paid better wages than they could get in smaller local firms which offered alternative employment prospects. They took the higher wages knowing this fact. They might not like the content of their work under the mass production system, but the choice was working elsewhere for less money. The behaviour of these men only made sense, therefore, as a trade-off: high consumption standards for brutalising and unrewarding work (Goldthorpe et al., 1969, p.182)

FLEXIBILITY AND SUBSTITUTABILITY OF LABOUR

Mass production is not a flexible system of production. It achieves high productivity by detailed management planning of work tasks, layout and sequencing of operations, and by ensuring a high and continuous level of effort by employees. Reorganising and retooling assembly lines for product changes is very expensive and time consuming, and thus such changes are relatively infrequent.

Paradoxically managers in mass production firms expect labour to be very 'flexible'. We have to be careful here to explain what flexibility means in the context of mass production systems. It means that management regard any normal, fit manual labour as being capable of being put to work at any of a wide variety of assembly line jobs. Of course this is only technically realistic because of the nature of most jobs found in mass production firms. These jobs require very little specialised skill and training. They are meant to be this way. The work has been planned 'scientifically' by management so that the worker is required merely to repeat a limited range of actions in a set way very intensively. In short, workers are flexible because they need minimal technical training under mass production and are, technically speaking, easily switched from one factory to another, indeed from one job to another. As a result, labour is not only flexible, it is also substitutable. In these circumstances, flexibility is the same as substitutability.

The emphasis on substitutable labour places a premium on minimal creativity by the worker. Any workers who tried to exercise intiative and express themselves through their work would wreck this system of working. To express this another way, labour is treated as labour in general rather than made up of specific types of labour. It is therefore seen mainly in quantitative terms: labour is either in short supply or surplus to requirements – the quality (above a certain minimal level of fitness and dexterity) and individual differences of labour are ignored and treated as unimportant.

This conception of labour under mass production – as general labour, as labour which is atomised, identical, substitutable units – is the source of concern about labour mobility. Since its individual quality does not matter and labour is regarded as more or less uniform – after all the mechanised assembly line allows no individual variations – all that matters is that such labour should go where it is needed in the right quantities. If it does not, then there is a lack of labour mobility.

But why should individuals want to cooperate with a system that wants them to suppress their own individuality? Why should they show a willingness to go wherever labour is most needed and to keep on working there for as long as needed? There is potentially a problem here. 'One of the main concerns of factory management is to gain a high commitment to the goals of management' (Tillett et al.,1970, p.34). Under mass production this commitment is sought via the level of wages.

High pay of mass-production workers reflects not high skill but high effort and flexibility. This high pay is the economic price management is prepared to pay in order to treat labour as maximally substitutable. But there is a social price for labour. It must work without any recognition of this activity as in accordance with its individuality, and thus without recognition of its own individual needs. In short, labour must not carry out the work *for* the worker: the worker must identify completely with working for the employer. That is, must be completely flexible and substitutable.

FORDISM AS A TOTALITY

The separate spheres of life – work, home, social and political – of the mass production worker may be seen as adding up to a whole. Blauner (1964) for instance, in describing the American car worker, put it all together as 'mass society'. Simplistically, mass society is where production is mass production and consumption is mass consumption.

But it does not stop there. Mass consumption involves mass markets, which are created and sustained by consumer credit. And somewhere along the line develops the welfare state, necessary to maintain peace in the mass society. For some, the growth of Keynesian welfare state provision, and state recognition of trade unions in pay bargaining and public policy making, together may be seen as institutional supports in the advanced capitalist democracy – mass society by another name – which work through the reduction of conflict (Offe, 1984, p.147).

THE CULTURE OF STRUGGLE IN MASS PRODUCTION

Under mass production, the limit of labour's flexibility (and therefore its substitutability) was established through trade union action. The brutal imposition of management control under mass production systems, and the limited capacity of 'high' wages to secure labour's total consent to it, evoked labour's resistance. The inevitability of this resistance rested on the fact that, however much workers might take a job for instrumental reasons, the use of their labour power could not be divorced from their *experience* of this use. In short, no matter how good the pay, the workers knew they were being pushed to their physical limits by this rationalised system of working.

The destructive nature of mass production systems of work was apparent from the earliest days of its application in Britain. The intense pace of the assembly line was still a problem in the 1960s and 1970s. Beynon reports the following words of a Ford shop steward:

> I never thought I'd survive. I used to come home from work and fall straight asleep. My legs and arms used to be burning. And I knew hard work. I'd been on the buildings but this place was a bastard then. (Beynon, 1973, p.75)

The brutality could reach extreme limits. On one occasion, according to Beynon, one man of about forty years, died by the side of the line, as his workmates were ordered back to work on the line. They were working as he lay dead (Beynon, 1973, p.76).

Labour fought back against the conditions of mass production. Huw Beynon's book, *Working For Ford*, is all about this struggle in the Ford factories in Liverpool and Dagenham.

> These plants have been dominated by skirmishes and a number of protracted confrontations between the workers and the employers. The car workers have been at the centre of the class struggle, yet the struggle has never extended beyond 'guerilla war'. Trade unionism has dominated the way the workers have conducted their struggles and the lessons they have learned from them. They have struggled bravely, and their resolve has frequently demanded admiration. (Beynon, 1973, p.317)

As his and other accounts show, the car workers in the mass production factories of the 1950s through to the 1970s struggled to improve their pay, to control the speed of the assembly line, to ensure safe working methods against management indifference, to ensure that overtime was fairly allocated, and to get treated like human beings and not just 'pairs of hands'.

Of course it took time before the workers of the car industry became organised and conducted the open struggles and skirmishes of which Beynon wrote. The semi-skilled workers who entered the car industry in the 1920s and 30s were for a long time unorganised. But despite employer opposition trade unionism was built up. And after the second world war, the record of strikes in the car industry showed signs of the increasing industrial conflict within the industry. 'Measured in customary terms of the ratio of 'lost' working days to the total of employees, therefore, the strike-incidence of the car firms has risen from about twice the national average in the early post-war years (a proportion by no means remarkable for manufacturing industry) to about six times the national average during the 1960s – thus contributing substantially to the rise in the national incidence itself (Turner et al., 1967, p.24). By the late 1960s, the vehicle industry was the most strike prone industry in manufacturing (Cronin, 1979: p.167).

THE NEW RIGHT AND THE CULTURE OF LABOUR

As we have seen in Chapter 6, the New Right saw trade unionism as not about workers seeking to protect themselves from over-work or ruinous working intensity, but about restrictions on competition in the labour market. In their terminology, they saw unions as the source of inflexibility in the labour market.

What is trade union restrictionism? According to Sir Keith Joseph the faults of trade unionism are, in effect, a lack of self-restraint. Thus, in the 1970s, he accused them of ignoring restraint because they believed the Government would bale them out. He said: 'Unions could afford to ignore restraint, not only in wage demands, but also in opposition to efficiency, in frivolity and cantankerousness, in anti-management luddism, in opposing modernisation' (Joseph, 1978, pp.103–4).

How could the New Right arrive at such diametrically opposed conclusions to those of writers such as Beynon? One answer might be that the New Right never empirically investigated the real life situation of trade unionism, never undertook detailed studies of real people in real workplaces. Their analyses were either couched in terms of sweeping historical generalisations or based on theoretical ideas about market forces and the role of trade unions according to the theories of orthodox economics.

The answer which the New Right came to was the demand for more labour market flexibility. Workers were exhorted to be more flexible about where they worked, when they worked and how they worked. It was a call for activity by labour to be confined entirely within the bounds of that required by employers. Absolute flexibility means labour activity totally *for* the employer.

This idea – flexibility – taken to its limit implies the absolute devaluing of labour activity to workers themselves. For the only person that matters in this idea is the employer. Labour is only of use to the extent that it is in the right place, at the right time, doing the right thing

– with right being defined by the employer – and thus only of use if totally serving the purposes of the employer.

To some extent, these New Right ideas on trade unionism and the importance of flexibility, especially labour market flexibility (mobility), can be seen as natural products of the period of mass production.

INTERNATIONAL COMPETITION

As far as the 1970s and 1980s were concerned, the dominant economic meaning of Post-Fordism for British capital was the defeat of indigenous mass production firms by overseas competition. The output figures tell the economic story clearly enough: the fast growth rates of manufacturing in the 1950s and 60s were replaced by contraction for the decade commencing 1973. And the fast growth of the British economy's GDP from 1951 to 1973 was succeeded by first a slowing down, and then a negligible growth in GDP between 1979 and 1983 (Meegan, 1988, p.154). So the mass production industries failed, and so did manufacturing generally, and along with them the whole economy suffered.

The technological case for 'Post-Fordism' merits careful appraisal with regard to Britain. On the one hand, the extent of mass production using assembly lines was by the 1980s very limited: one estimate for the early 1980s suggested that there were only 700 000 assembly line workers in Britain (Meegan, 1988, p.157). And in 1986 it seems only about 16 per cent of manufacturing plants had mechanically paced assembly lines (ibid, p.157). On the other hand, the use of microprocessors, essential in the technological conceptions of Post-Fordism, whilst growing fast was still very limited by the mid-1980s. The Policy Studies Institute found that in 1985 between roughly 40 and 80 per cent of UK factories were using processes incorporating microelectronics, with the percentage varying according to the industry. The types of equipment most commonly used in the factories were programmable logic controllers, computer numerically controlled machine tools, and computer aided design work stations (Daniel, 1987, p.3). This did not add up to computer controlled factories. In 1985 a group of consultant engineers apparently could not locate a single genuine example of computer-integrated manufacturing (Meegan, 1988, pp.170–1).

Further evidence suggests that Britain is lagging behind in the movement towards a hi-tech future. The study by Steedman and

Wagner (1987), to which we referred in an earlier chapter, found massive differences between West German and British firms manufacturing fitted kitchens in 1986–7. Most importantly the German factories were automated to a much greater extent, with even very small ones having computer numerically controlled woodworking machinery. The German factories also made extensivè use of automatic feed and automatic offload, and had formed complex machine lines five or ten years earlier. But 'in Britain, on the other hand, fully linked machine lines with automatic feed and automatic offload were hardly to be seen in the plants we visited' (Steedman and Wagner, 1987, p.88).

The German firms' investment in CNC machinery enabled them to make competitively priced and 'tailor-made' products. This was based on the flexibility that the technology offered. The British firms had apparently held back from linked machinery in order to achieve a different type of flexibilty. For the British firms, flexibility 'referred to the need to *interrupt* planned production to 'rush through' small special batches – sometimes referred to as 'balances' or 'shortages' – which were urgently required to complete an order which was otherwise being met from stock, or met from a batch specially produced but not to a precise count' (ibid., p.88). Steedman and Wagner commented that the German companies gained in terms of better plant utilisation and fewer frayed nerves.

JAPANESE MANAGEMENT IN BRITAIN

A number of well known Japanese companies took over or set up factories in Britain during the 1980s. They caused quite a stir and their progress and performance has been closely watched. The first well known example of Japanese management in action involved Toshiba and the EETPU in 1981. The management and union negotiated an agreement which covered 300 employees at Toshiba's television factory in Plymouth. The agreement provided for single union recognition, single status terms and conditions, complete flexibility in the use of manpower, consultative arrangements involving a company advisory board of employees and management, and pendulum arbitration to resolve disputes (IRRR, 1984, No.324).

An agreement between Nissan and the AUEW covered the factory built at Washington, Tyne and Wear (Leese, 1985). It included provisions on a single union agreement, start of shift meetings, abandonment of traditional job descriptions, involvement of production workers in maintenance work, common terms of employment, and a special disputes procedure. The latter required disputes to be settled through a works council, which acted as both a consultative and a negotiating body, and then if not settled, to be referred to ACAS for conciliation, and finally to an optional pendulum arbitration stage.

In the case of Nissan Peter Wickens, the company's personnel director, emphasised teamwork as integral to the behaviour of Japanese workers when he said, at an Industrial Society conference, that his company had looked at the way Japanese workers conduct themselves day-to-day.

> One area which was immediately apparent was teamwork. The Japanese at all levels see themselves as part of a team. (Leese, 1985, p.326)

He suggested that the effect of Japanese employers fostering team spirit was to ensure that it was in the workers' own interests to be concerned with quality, getting the job right and keeping the working environment clean and tidy.

In the case of the agreement between Hitachi and the EETPU at the company's Hirwaun factory in 1984 and 85, the formal aims were described by management as being to get a speedier employee response to change, to facilitate a change towards job flexibility, and to get a consensus approach to conflict resolution. According to the company's personnel specialist, ideally the company was aiming at complete flexibility – employees contracted to perform whatever duties were within their capability whenever instructed to do so. The thinking here was that the company wanted a consensus approach to conflict resolution, with industrial action minimised (Pegge, 1986).

FLEXIBILITY AGAIN

It is immediately obvious that the typical Japanese package comprised a combination of flexible working and a more consensual approach to management–labour relations. Both require closer analysis. The flexibility is not the flexibility which was implicit in Fordised mass production.

For a start, the Japanese companies were not aiming at maximum substitutability of labour, they were aiming at maximum substitutability of labour *activity*. To put this another way, they did not want flexibility in their recruitment of labour, but they did want flexibility in the *use* of labour. Hence there is a strong commitment by Japanese companies in Britain to job security for employees. The Japanese offer long-term employment to the individual – they do not want to see them as mobile as possible in the labour market sense.

And this is where the emphasis on training and employees' willingness to respond to change comes in. The firms aim at flexible manufacturing and so jobs will change frequently. They want employees who will accept change readily and will be receptive to training. Indeed it has been suggested that firms with new ventures in Britain 'are increasingly weighting the 'social skills' of their workforces (essentially their receptiveness and malleability towards corporate goals) above more technical skills' (Meegan, 1988, p.148). This also explains why the Japanese approach rejects the use of detailed job descriptions – it is counterproductive from the point of view of adaptability of the workforce.

Single status agreements, which abolish or reduce differences in terms and conditions of employment between different strata of employees, start of shift meetings, consultative arrangements, consensual approaches to conflict resolution add up to a distinctive industrial relations approach – one that clearly aims at building a team or industrial community spirit.

The meaning of the employee relations moves by Japanese firms has been ascribed to various motives. Some commentators see the single union deals as evidence of anti-union attitudes – a 'new unitarism'. Or, the stress on consensual approaches to conflict resolution may be taken as a sign that they are not so much anti-union as anti-strikes.

At its base they strive against the view that company and workforce have interests which are polar opposites and for the company-as-a-community image. In Britain, on the whole they have worked on the basis of the union as a part of that community, involving the unions as partners in consultation and in conflict resolution. So on one hand the management seeks to reduce the awareness in labour of the need to oppose management's attempts to secure flexibility (management is not 'them' but part of 'us' who make up the factory community) and on the other, builds in the right of the union to have a say in company matters and how conflict is to be resolved. In short, they use ideas of community (embodied in material practice) and participation to gain commitment, and this stands in marked contrast to the use of high pay as in the Fordised approach.

The importance of their practices for the this analysis is that it shows that British management was not able to confront and deal with the contradiction between mass production's imposition of flexibility and the resistance of trade unionism. It could not see how it could respond to the nature of labour as a social process, how it could respond to labour's refusal to regard its activity as merely a means to an end. In short, they could not handle the idea of industry as a social system with social relations and social forces – they were locked into treating labour as an economic category.

Importantly the management approach which has triumphed – Japanese management – whilst remaining essentially exploitative, has shown itself to be superior in realising that labour has a social aspect that is neglected at capital's peril, and shows itself to be more aware of the need to develop labour as an active element in the economic process, conscious of the importance of labour being receptive to change and training. It also has shown, in Britain at least, a greater shrewdness about treating labour as collectively and individually important, as evidenced by the stress on consultation and employment security.

POST-FORDISM IN BRITAIN: FLEXIBILITY AND ALIENATION

Surveys covering industry in the 1980s found abundant evidence of managers attempting to introduce 'flexibilities'. One survey of large manufacturing plants during the early 1980s found that 43 per cent had introduced one or more types of increased flexibility in the period 1980–4 (Daniel, 1987). It seems that attempts had been made to relax demarcations between production and maintenance workers, and between different groups of craft workers; and there had been attempts to bring in new multi-skilled craftsmen and new enhanced craftsmen. These attempts were especially common in the larger establishments where there was slightly less flexibility.

This same survey pointed to the existence of quite extensive flexibilities by 1984. For example production workers were quite commonly involved in routine maintenance work, and it was very common to find them involved in the setting up of machines. Both of these activities have at times been jealously guarded by craft workers. The days of craft specialisation were also apparently passing: in more than half the cases for example, electricians were to be found doing mechanical fitting.

Further flexibilities were made, in manufacturing and elsewhere, during the mid 1980s, with production workers increasingly taking on routine maintenance work, craftsmen doing work usually performed by other craftsmen, and various other demarcations being relaxed and flexibilities being introduced (ACAS, 1988). There were also indications of the growth of 'flexible employment'. Many organisations were increasing their numbers of temporary workers and making more use of contractors. There was also some growth in the employment of part-timers (ACAS, 1988).

The growth of flexible employment could also be seen in official data. The Labour Force Survey of 1983 had found 68 per cent of people in employment were full-time permanent employees; by the time of the 1986 Survey this had fallen to 66 per cent (Hakim, 1987). The rest, the 'flexible workers', consisting of the self-employed, temporary workers, and part-time workers had thus become one-third of the employed labour force. In fact many – two thirds – of these flexible workers were part-timers. Many were women working in catering, cleaning, hairdressing and other personal service occupations; so it would be wrong to automatically associate this development with the reorganisation of production – the role of the structural shift from the male dominated manufacturing industries to the female dominated service industries has also to be considered as a possible explanation. Nevertheless, it was clear from a CBI survey in 1984 that many employers in manufacturing did intend to increase the extent of their contracted out services and their proportions of part-timers and temporary workers (Hakim, 1987).

So what are we to make of all this evidence? Has a new flexible economy been formed in the 1980s? The fact is that managers in Britain have always imposed flexible working where possible, and the mass unemployment and demoralised trade union thinking made it possible for managers to *force* through the flexibilities. There is no compelling evidence that *consent* to the changes had been created by British managers. And there was no evidence that the high pay policy of mass production–mass consumption society had been weakened as the source of the hegemony of the British industrial system.

ORGANISING FOR COMMITMENT

Some British companies have attempted to learn from the Japanese. The management of Thorn EMI Ferguson for example, visited Japan in the late 1970s and early 1980s (Taylor, 1984, p.279). They concluded that they had to compete in the field of employee commitment if they were to have a long term future.

There is however a credibility gap which is matched only by the discontent British labour feels in regard to the intrinsic nature of work and the working situation. According to the results of the Work and Society study published in 1984:

> The disparity . . . between what British workers expect from their jobs and what they actually get from them reveals them to be potentially one of the world's most discontented workforces. (Work and Society, 1984, p.54)

It found that a majority of British workers worked to improve their standard of living but few of these felt they were achieving their goal. Furthermore the study, which involved surveys of workers in the United States, Japan, West Germany, Sweden and Israel, as well as in Britain, found a relatively high incidence of 'bad jobs' in Britain. 'A "bad job" was defined as one that has low pay, little job security, little chance for advancement, and where workers are ashamed of the place where they work' (ibid., p.55). Great Britain had the highest percentage of bad jobs of the six countries studied – at a rate of over one in five.

The researchers made three very interesting points which are worth repeating here. Firstly, they emphasised the importance of making sure that reasonable numbers of workers found their jobs interesting, challenging or rewarding. They quoted Michael Shanks, who had been the programme director of Work and Society, as saying that British management had perhaps not taken on board what it was that British workers now expected. Secondly, they argued that non-economic incentives were needed to motivate commitment by the workforce, that pay cheques had to be balanced by psychic rewards, and that people needed various things from jobs, including challenge, the development of new skills, social interaction, etcetera. They argued that competitive success might depend on getting this balance of psychic as well as pay rewards. And they considered that 'The job itself would have to be improved before a dissatisfied worker is likely to be transformed into a committed one' (ibid., 1984, p.55). Thirdly, they seemed to credit Japanese management with a good record in their treatment of employees. At least, they quoted Pehr Gyllenhammer, Chairman of Volvo, at length, who made this point.

> 'It is rather surprising,' he remarked, 'that people representing democracies with constitutions protecting individual freedom and

human rights have to go to Japan – which had its constitution and democracy forced upon it by the Allies – to find out how to treat people. It seems to me that we are up for a cultural shock.' (ibid., 1984, p.55)

Given the failure of British managers to develop intrinsically or socially rewarding work, there is no sign that high pay has been reduced as the employers' basic method of achieving hegemony. It is therefore interesting that the repeated calls by the Thatcher administrations to slow down the rise in earnings in order to bring down unemployment have been ignored. Why should this be? Could it be that if employers had listened and resisted pay increases, they would have been left without any significant means of maintaining workforce commitment?

PRODUCTION AND POLITICAL IDEAS IN THE 1980S

The message of Thatcherism in the 1980s was that the labour market was now starting to work more efficiently, and that the destructive power of the unions had been dealt with, but that pay was still rising too fast. In fact the political ideas of Thatcherism on the economy lumbered along behind the realities of production, probably because the starting point was a theoretical one, rather than the realities of production and its social relations. Only at the very end of the decade was Thatcherism anywhere near glimpsing the real problems of the British economy which lay not in the labour market, or any other market, but in production itself.

In 1979 and 1980, at the beginning of the Thatcher experiment, as it has been called, the Government said it was primarily concerned about monetary policy and the economy. The policy was – literally from beginning to end – to make sure that money was alright. By getting money supply under good control the Government would begin to bring about its declared end of preserving the value of money, that is of eliminating inflation. But, in explaining how this policy of controlling the money supply achieved lower inflation, labour had to be brought into the reckoning as part of the process through which a good money supply would turn into low inflation. At this stage in the Government's thinking it seemed, from what it said, that the *only* important thing about labour was how much it was paid in wages and salaries. That is, it seemed as though the Government only regarded labour from the point of view of how much money it received. It said that if wages and salaries rose too much then unemployment would rise and the adjustment to the new money supply conditions would be delayed and difficult. Accordingly the key message from Government was directed to pay negotiators: they were warned that they were choosing between pay moderation and high unemployment.

After a few years it was noticable that labour had stopped being an intervening variable between monetary policy and inflation and had become instead a 'supply side' variable which the Government wished to affect in its crusade to make 'markets work better'. In the process, the Government thinking seemed to have moved from the macro-economy down to the micro-economy. Thus instead of using the economy's money supply to sort out the economy's inflation, the object of their economic ministrations was now the market, or more precisely the various markets which were seen as over-regulated and over-controlled.

This phase of Government thinking implied a much more active Thatcherite policy. They were now after a 'flexible economy'. They were after growth and jobs without inflation. And the flexible economy was going to deliver these things. The flexible economy, as befits a concept which was associated with a crusade to make markets work better, was one where people responded speedily to changing market demands. Perhaps this can be seen as the obverse of the first phase of thinking where it was assumed that the right response would eventually be delivered. In that first phase, pay negotiators and others had to choose how they were going to adjust to the market conditions created by a good control of the money supply, but sooner or later they were supposed to choose what the market demanded – lower pay rises. However, labour was still regarded primarily as wages and salaries.

Simultaneously, Government thinking in this 'middle' period showed signs of developing a more complex view of labour. First, changes in taxation and unemployment benefits were justified in terms of the need to make paid employment a more attractive option as compared to unemployment. Secondly, the encouragement of profit sharing and share option schemes was justified in terms of the need to tie in the commitment of the worker to that of the private employer. These were interesting developments in Government policy and thinking because they represented a view of the need to get labour to work, whereas before this time the Government seemed to have been preoccupied with limiting the monetary rewards of labour. However the thinking at this stage had not progressed beyond that idea of labour as a financial transaction, albeit one that some people had to be encouraged more strongly to make (the unemployed) and one that other people needed to be encouraged to make in greater concert with employers (those who were eligible for profit sharing and share option schemes).

For labour, the flexible economy of Government thinking had very few implications in the production sphere. It was mainly in the labour market where labour was going to be flexible, which meant being prepared to take jobs and being prepared to change them when the market demanded it. Being inflexible meant producing unemployment.

In the late 1980s Government thinking started to locate labour in the 'enterprise economy'. This enterprise economy was the flexible economy, but it was more than that, for it incorporated an important additional idea. This extra concept was one of a 'souped' up enterprising attitude amongst employers. The Government explained that it was not merely taking measures to improve the supply side of markets, it was also stimulating enterprise.

This third phase of thinking was most apparent in the Enterprise Initiative of Lord Young. The Department of Trade and Initiative became the Department for Enterprise. This meant that the Government was going to champion the people who make things happen – the entrepreneurs.

From the breadth of the Enterprise Initiative it seems that Government had the idea that there was a lot wrong with British business. But Government statements and policies at the close of the 1980s suggested two areas of weakness which had important implications for British labour. Firstly, it seems that the Government arrived at the idea that employers needed to invest more in the training of workers. Secondly, there were hints that the Government thought employers had failed to build constructive industrial relations. The Employment Department's *Employment for the 1990s* announced that labour was the key *resource*. In other words, in this White Paper labour graduated from being wages and salaries to being the key resource – in terms of Government thinking labour had finally moved out of the labour market and into the sphere of production. With this step forward, the Government, or rather one Department of it, acknowledged the importance of social relations in production:

> The challenge for employers is to involve their staff directly in the economic success of their businesses. (Employment Department, 1988, p.17)

In addition this recognition of the importance of employee involvement accompanied a new awareness of the particularity of British trade unionism. Whilst British unions may still be seen as important only for restrictive practices, stoppages, and excessive pay settlements, the Government by the end of the 1980s allowed that some unions can enjoy constructive relations with employers and contribute to productivity growth.

Implicitly this Government thinking at the end of the 1980s hints at a conclusion which is directly the opposite of that which lay at the heart of its thinking of ten years earlier. That conclusion is that labour must be valued – by training it and by building commitment through employee involvement. Ten years earlier the Government's thinking had begun with money and ended with the aim of valuing money, and considered labour only as temporary possessor of money (wages and salaries) not as something that needed to be valued for itself.

Part III
Critique and Policy

We have reached the moment in our analysis of the cultural development of labour when the empirical evidence and discussion of policy, which we have been examining in earlier chapters, must develop into a comprehensive understanding of the particular experience of labour. This requires that we develop analytically, firstly, the major processes which construct the whole experience of labour, and secondly, the conditions which affect the relationships between the processes. The clarification and definition of the relevant processes and conditions occupies the first chapter of the third part of this book.

This is only the first step in constructing an analysis of the cultural development of labour as a totality. For the results of the major processes are contingent on the *specific* conditions which prevail in Britain today. Therefore in the subsequent chapter the contemporary conditions of Britain are examined with the aim of identifying the sources of the crises in the development of labour. We bring out in precise terms the social and cultural factors which are obstructing and suppressing the growth of skills, knowledge and competence amongst Britain's workers, and thereby preventing the development of a high quality and productive workforce.

In the last chapter, the analysis of the development of British labour, and of the crises which characterise labour in Britain, is taken forward into an analysis of policies for raising the quality and productiveness of labour. This will be looking to ways of overcoming the current limitations on labour's long-term growth and development, as well as the steps necessary to tackle the immediate crises in Britain's employment policies.

8 Understanding the General Social Conditions of Production

INTRODUCTION

In this chapter we set out the basic concepts which, in subsequent chapters, are used to analyse the cultural development of labour in Britain and provide an analysis on which to base policy recommendations for employment policy.

We begin by defining the nature of labour. This is followed by an analysis of the major processes which lead to changes and developments in labour. On the foundations of an understanding of these processes we explore the conditions which are necessarily important in the way in which these processes are articulated one with another.

THE NATURE OF LABOUR

The immediate answer to the question of 'What is labour?' is that it is an activity. It is an activity which results in useful products or services. And it is an activity which is absolutely necessary if the human race is to survive, since as human beings we have some needs which are essential to our survival, and which will only be met if labour occurs.

All this is immediately obvious to most people. Equally obvious is that the content of labour changes and continues to change. Government statistics show that Great Britain's occupied workforce in 1841 consisted largely of men and women working in agriculture, manufacturing and services, with those working in services being largely composed of a massive army of female domestic servants (Mitchell, 1978). As late as 1851 one in four men aged over 20 were farmworkers and, according to Tony Lane, one in six of the occupied population from 1871 to 1891 were 'in service' (Lane, 1974). In 1971 economically active men and women worked mainly in manufacturing, commerce and finance, and services, with very few of those in services working as domestic servants. So in the intervening years the numbers of people in agricultural occupations had dwindled, whilst the numbers in commerce and finance occupations had mushroomed, and those in service occupations were no longer domestic servants.

The detailed content of labour has also changed. This has been due in part to organisational changes. The arrival in the Britain of the 1930s of 'Fordised' factories, based on organisation for mass production, meant that workers in manufacturing industries increasingly found themselves working at a speed, and to a tempo, completely set by machinery. The rationalised content of work and the speed of working placed workers under qualitatively new stresses, ones that older workers found difficult to endure (Cole, 1933, p.25).

Recent scientific and technological advances have been accompanied by an increase in the number of professionals and others in science and technology. In the spring of 1988, 4.23 per cent of all people in employment in Great Britain were in professional and related occupations in science, engineering, technology and similar fields (Department of Employment, 1989).

It is obvious that the changes in labour activity which we have noted call for changes in people themselves. The physical and mental abilities, as well as the mentality and nervous energy, of people working as farm labourers or domestic servants in the middle of the 19th century are entirely different from those of men and women working in a robotised factory or a commercial or financial organisation towards the close of the 20th century. The separation in the material and cultural way of life of these two periods is equally distinct.

LABOUR IS ALSO SOCIETY

This book rests on understanding the essential duality of labour. On the one hand it is an economic activity – engaged in both production and, in a different location, consumption. But on the other hand, it is *at the same time* also social, engaged in relationships that are not simply economic. Much of the problem of understanding this duality stems from the powerful ideological and social split between the *economic* and the *social* in capitalist society.

This separation is endemic. Most of us experience work as a different sphere from home life. For very many, the two are opposed. Most people see their family life as something to be protected from work. There is considerable evidence that this split resolves itself in very distinctive gender differences. Even when men and women in a family structure both work the man will engage in domestic labour to a much smaller extent than the woman. The world of work is *still* understood as essentially male, and the world of the home as essentially female. Given these gender differences it is important to note, as we do both earlier in the book and later on, that it has been modern feminist thought and ideas that have become one of the very few strands of social thought capable of the responsibility of bringing both the spheres of work and the home together.

The separation exists intellectually with very few intellectuals trying to work in both the understanding of economic production and social relations outside of work. Economists talk a different language, think different thoughts and worry about different things (just what *is* a sick pound?). Those interested in the social sphere also have different languages and concerns, and can develop specific interests which seem to misunderstand the importance of economic production and human labour.

As we shall see in the next chapter, the Thatcherite experiment was responsible for viewing economic and social relations in an entirely different way. Within their ideology, the power of the market as the determining influence could not be universal. It stopped at the front door, or at least at the bedroom, where the different ideologies of family relations, personal responsibilities, care and even a little love, were the order of the day. No Government Minister in the 1980s ever suggested buying and selling children or other family relations. In fact when it came to the care of the elderly, the very *un*market mechanism of the way in which children should look after their parents stressed the *lack of economic* relations and the dominance of care and duty within this aspect of Government ideology.

We pose against these powerful social, intellectual and political bifurcations the obvious reality that the people in the home, within the family, engaged in leisure, watching TV and thinking through their politics, are the *same* people who go out to work, and think that it probably is not worth their while retraining, or do not feel like doing the overtime this year to consume that holiday. These worlds are interlinked by the lives of the people who live them. Any understanding that sunders these two worlds will fail.

At one obvious level in the 1850s mentioned above, the dangerous sanitary conditions of home life ensured that many workers turned up to the world of work sick and feeble. This was reciprocated by a dangerous world of work that would push back a worker towards home enfeebled by industrial diseases and injuries. The pathological world of the home made them sick workers; the dangerous world of work made them injured social human beings. Within this chapter we will argue that the problems being experienced by the cultural production of labour can only be explained by the joint analysis of the economic and the social. Whilst much of what we have to say explores the conceptual framework within the sphere of production and consumption, there are other vital contradictions that exist because too many economists and politicians forget that labour is also society.

PRODUCING AND CONSUMING

Why does labour as an activity change? Workers are little involved in the strategic decisions of their employing organisations. Furthermore studies of British industries show that most organisational and technical change is planned and introduced by managers. Very rarely are employees involved in the decisions on change – certainly change is rarely negotiated with employees or their union representatives and consultation occurs mainly either where there are unions or, in the minority of cases, where change is unpopular and workers are not in favour of it (Daniel, 1987). So it seems labour as an activity changes because management wants it to and sees a need for it.

Why do managers want changes in labour and why do they see a need for it? For private sector managers the answer might be given that they organise labour activity, and change it, in order to produce what consumers demand. So it seems that ultimately consumption dictates the changes in labour as an activity. But consumers choose to consume products and services from amongst those available. So their demand is constructed within limits set by what is produced. Of course there may be a certain shifting of production of goods and services to better match what is demanded, and a switching of demand as production is changed to reflect demand. But in the end the production of goods and services would match the pattern of demand from consumers and the whole system would cease to develop.

Analytically speaking, we therefore seem unable to explain the continuing dynamism of labour as an activity just by reference to the processes internal to production and consumption.

A TYPOLOGY OF BASIC PROCESSES

Production and consumption are connected by other processes. These consist of simple circulation, social distribution and the social relationships of the whole of society. So, the whole sequence of processes consists of:

(1) the world of work where the production process takes place and where workers produce goods and services.

(2) the simple circulation process which comprises the payment of wages and salaries to employees and the purchase of goods and services by them, and which takes place in the social world constructed away from the world of work.

(3) the political and social distribution processes, where some of the surplus profit and pay is turned into tax revenue, allocations are made to citizens of goods and services, and there is the payment of social security.

(4) the social consumption process in which workers and their families consume goods and services within the wider world.

(5) the social world where labour is produced and reproduced, and where consumption takes place.

It is within these very different processes, tied together through the nature of labour, that the cultural production of labour occurs.

THE PRODUCTION PROCESS AND THE SOCIAL WORLD OF WORK

Labour activity occurs within the context of production. In Western democracies we immediately think of this in terms of paid employment, either in the the production of commodities (goods or services) which are distributed through the market mechanism, or in the production of non-marketed goods as in the case of public services paid for out of taxation. Domestic unpaid labour activity also forms a major part of production in modern societies, albeit often unrecognised. Where production for the market occurs, labour activity also leads to the formation of profit.

In defining the nature of the production process, it is sometimes emphasised that work under capitalistic systems is inevitably monotonous and boring. This may result from a false identification of capitalist production with mass production, a form of organisation of work which is currently showing signs of being superceded.

However, based on images of work derived from the mass production scenario, it may be argued that some historic forms of production (namely, capitalistic ones) are essentially defined by the characteristic that work is for the worker merely a means to an end. This definition of the production process under capitalism is too one-sided. Following Offe, it is important to recognise 'investive' and 'consumptive' elements within labour activity – even in the capitalistic system. Workers, he says, are never fully divorced from the concrete process of the utilization of their labour power by employers (Offe, 1984, p.233). Workers do not only invest effort in return for income, they also 'consume' whilst at work, that is, to some degree experience work as meeting their needs. It might be emphasised that workers *experience* work – their needs, emotions, humanity, etc., are not switched off simply because they are at work – even if they themselves define their primary motivation as being to reap the maximum financial rewards for the energy they are required to expend. Accordingly a definition of the production process which posited work as only a means to an end for workers would have to be criticised as one-sided, and therefore not completely true.

Work, experienced within the boundaries of a capitalist society, will always contain an element that consists of activity as a simple means to an end. It will do so because so many of the social and economic arrangements that both surround and imbue the world of work stress that particular theme of experience. This has been recognised by Heilbroner who argues that under capitalism the act of labour is not valued:

A business civilization regards work as a means to an end, not as an end in itself. The end is profit, income, consumption, economic growth, or whatever; but the act of labour itself is regarded as nothing more than an unfortunate necessity to which we must submit to obtain this end. (Heilbroner, 1976, p.90)

The experience of work as a means to an end also results from the separation mentioned above between labour as an activity and the organisation of that activity to create production. Very few of those engaged in labour are also engaged in its organisation, so a simple experience of alienation will follow.

We stress that despite that alienation, despite the economic and cultural pressure to see the world of work simply as a means to an end, there are a wealth of other experiences actually and potentially contained within it that are not simply means to ends. These include the collective relationship missing from the world of unemployment and much domestic labour, the wider necessary organisation of working with others and the struggle against alienation and expropriation. All these ends are in themselves experiential and all are to be gained from the world of work.

It is a crucial part of our argument that when the world of work is denuded of these experiences, when it is reduced primarily to a means-to-an-end experience, it becomes one that is less welcoming to people outside of it. If work is *only* a means to an end, and if that end can be obtained elsewhere, then its activity diminishes to zero. It follows therefore that in a society where there are alternatives to working as a means-to-an-end, then it is *essential* that the world of work stresses the importance of those other real ends in themselves. Otherwise, people will not go to work.

SIMPLE CIRCULATION

The simple circulation process involves the payment of wages and salaries to employees, and the use of this income by them to purchase commodities.

Pay differentials are found in all modern societies and are usually assumed to reflect differences in skill, knowledge and productivity. They also reflect social organisation.

The commodities purchased include items which enable employees to maintain themselves and their families (that is 'necessaries') and other items which are generally regarded as outside of current definitions of the indispensable ('luxuries'). These definitions are socially constructed.

There is a historical element in the determination of the boundary between necessaries and luxuries, with items in the latter category constantly moving into the category of the necessary. There is also a constant tendency for the category of the luxury item to be replenished by the creation of new commodities. This adds up to a rising material standard of living for waged and salaried employees. It is also one of the keys to understanding the dynamism in labour activity itself, and will receive further attention below.

The definition of necessaries is partly determined by the specific nature of the employee's labour activity. People doing heavy manual work, or work requiring intensive inputs of energy for instance, are prone to purchase food with a high carbohydrate content. Certain types of clothing are required by those engaged in office and commercial activity.

The changing historical nature of individual and family purchasing patterns is reflected in the revisions in the cost of living indexes used by governments. In the late twentieth century however, typical families in advanced capitalist countries spent the bulk of their money on housing, food, transport and vehicles, fuel, light and power, and clothing and footwear.

POLITICAL AND SOCIAL DISTRIBUTION PROCESSES

The concept of social distribution must be differentiated from that of state intervention in the economy. The latter includes the situation where the state intervenes, by means of regulatory activity, in production and simple circulation, as well as in taking care of the national defence and law and order. Where social distribution is extensive, then the state is again substantially involved in the sphere of economic relations. But the specific processes making up social distribution include the public allocation of certain non-marketed goods and services, the provision of social security to enable some groups of citizens to increase their share of the commodities purchased through the market, and the collection of state revenue through taxation to fund these state activities.

The non-marketed goods and services allocated by the state to its citizens include health services, education and other social services. Social security, consisting of money allocated by the state to individuals and families, is directed towards the unemployed, retired persons, sick and disabled people, low income families, and families with dependent children. The redistributive element in taxation and public allocation is the result of society's desire to modify the distribution of income and wealth determined by decisions under the control of private individuals.

The character of social distribution as a whole process can be viewed in economic, legal or social terms. An economic view of the role of social distribution pinpoints the need of the capitalist system, which is very anarchic, to generate state planning as a process modifying and supporting capitalist production. Generally speaking, this suggests the importance of the concept of 'organised capitalism' in contradistinction to that of 'laissez-faire capitalism' (Cole, 1933, p.511). Whilst this identifies the development of state regulation for the whole of the capitalistic sector of the economy, the specific character of social distribution processes relate to the need for capital to compete internationally on the basis of a healthy, well-educated and socially adjusted national workforce.

The legal perspective emphasises the growth of legal rights for workers under welfare state capitalism, which means rights to free public health services, free public education, and to minimum standards of living. Socially, the growth of social distribution may be taken as broadly bringing about a society in which the common person has come into their own, when all have an equal chance of the good life, and there are no gross disparities in wealth and income.

Social distribution, like simple circulation, provides a key to the changes in labour activity. Historically its importance has become established more recently than that of simple circulation, but international trading conditions have conspired to enlarge the role of the state in what is sometimes referred to as the reproduction of labour power, and this has entailed an expansion of social distribution. The whole process of social distribution is examined below, and its connection to simple circulation raised.

It should be stressed though that the essential nature of social distribution is *political*. Different groups in society struggle in very different ways to gain influence over the extent of social distribution and the way in which it is carried out. Even recent political history from the 1960s to the present day demonstrates that one of the main aims of politics is to change the proportion of social money distributed and the way in which it is distributed.

Theoretically this is an important issue since it stresses the fact that workers are not simply the *recipients* of this distribution in a passive but grateful way, but in a democratic society play a role in the struggles over that distribution. Of course there are a wide variety of different ways in which they play that role. An 'apolitical', 'passive' citizen who does not even vote and submissively consumes whatever is distributed will have little activity; but a woman who is an active trade unionist, plays a role in both a political party and voluntary organisations, combined with her pre-eminent role in the domestic sphere, would be of very great significance as an active engagement in politics as well as having little leisure time for herself!

Thus the political sphere for labour – their role as citizens and how they carry out that role – plays an active part in this process of social distribution.

CONSUMPTION

The concept of consumption is defined as the process whereby individuals meet their various and complex needs. The most obvious ones, namely food, shelter and warmth, involve the using up of goods and services which have been obtained via simple circulation or social distribution.

The concept of consumption is sometimes reduced to that of reproduction of labour power. According to this definition of consumption, the capacity of workers to labour is used up during the production process and consumption is then required if the capacity to labour is to be formed once again. Further, it is posited that the wages and salaries paid to workers in exchange for their expenditure of energy in working, is sufficient to purchase goods and services to enable this restoration of labour power, but not enough to enable workers to avoid having to work for a living (that is labour is forced into commodification of its labour power).

The concept of the reproduction of labour power is usually defined as including actual reproduction of human beings (that is the procreation and rearing of children) to form the replacement and expansion of labour power needed by capitalist employers. It may be defined as involving publicly provided services and requiring the labour of doctors, nurses, teachers and other public service workers.

The definition of consumption as simply reproduction of labour power is false however. People take part in consumption not only in order to reproduce their labour power, but also to meet their own needs. Indeed the immediate impression most people have of consumption is that it is something that individuals do for their own gratification. It is only critical reflection which suggests that individuals also consume for their employers, so that employers have the use of fit and healthy labour power.

The falsity, or rather one-sidedness, of the concept of consumption as simply the reproduction of labour power is also due to the necessity of work, and not just consumption for the reproduction of labour power. Indeed the scale of domestic, unpaid labour, mainly by women, exceeds the scale of paid work (Greater London Council, 1985, p.19).

Finally, an essential aspect of individual consumption is its involvement with pursuits and activities which take place in 'spare time'. Spare time is time which individuals are really free to dispose of as they wish; it is not time which is used for reproduction of labour power (for example, cleaning, cooking and caring for children).

Consumption is therefore in part oriented to developing physical, mental, artistic and other individual qualities, as opposed to just restoring or recuperating the individual's vitality. Examples of individual development activities taking place in spare time include the use of cultural and educational opportunities presented by television and tourism, the use of sports facilties, and the use of social facilties such as leisure complexes with restaurants, cinemas, and opportunities for bowling, snooker and ice skating.

The point we are stressing here is that whether we use the concept of consumption or reproduction, this is an *active* process. One that involves citizens – who may be labour in another context – playing an active role in the consumption of goods and services, or an active role in their leisure activities or spare time, or – even more importantly – an active role with their families and children and their socialisation.

In stressing this activity we recognise that we are disagreeing with a powerful political view of the role of consumption, which spans such important works as Vance Packard's 1950s work on advertising (*The Hidden Persuaders*), Herbert Marcuse's *One Dimensional Man*, and a whole host of texts stressing the functional nature of reproduction and consumption within capitalism.

Of course the advertising industry plays a powerful role in channelling and trying to form patterns of consumption. As Galbraith says, advertising is the management of consumer demand:

> The control or management of demand is, in fact, a vast and rapidly growing industry in itself. It embraces a huge network of communications, a great array of merchandising and selling organisations, nearly the entire advertising industry, numerous ancillary research, training and other related services and much more. In everyday parlance this great machine, and the demanding and varied talents that it employs, are said to be engaged in selling goods. In less ambiguous language it means that it is engaged in the management of those who buy goods. (Galbraith, 1967, pp.204–5)

Subsequent years have increased the size of this sector considerably. Even in 1966 Baran and Sweezy were undoubtedly correct when they said that 'advertising has turned into an indispensable tool for a large sector of corporate business' (Baran and Sweezy, 1966, p.123). Advertising does set out to manipulate the motivation of consumers, to create new wants, and stimulate others, and to change life-styles; it is not just a matter of drawing the attention of consumers to products.

Yet the size of the advertising sector, and the skills and dexterity of their work in the enormous task of creating and recreating society, demonstrates over and over again that it is not totally possible. There are grave difficulties in seeing such industries as simply making the world since that one dimensional power process excludes the development of grave difficulties caused by people's ideas, experiences and different hopes. All we are claiming is that the one-sided view of the social power of advertising is simply that – one-sided. It is necessary to view the role of the active consumer.

Of course, we are aware of the literature on 19th century leisure which stresses the way in which different economic and political forces tried to channel past spare time activities (Thompson, 1980). But that simple functional view of the way working people submit to external organisation is undermined by the active way in which they choose to construct their own leisure activities – or at the very least to construct their own methods of working at leisure within the structures on offer. In short, no-one can chart exactly why *Eastenders* became more popular than *Coronation Street* in 1988 – it was not planned from the top.

The ability of advertising to make people to order, then, has limits. There may be a 'relentless effort' by advertising to get people to change their life style and wants in order to sell the products of capitalism, but it has to deal with a consumer who is far from a passive and helpless victim, and far from naive. Indeed part of the 'taken for granted' knowledge of the typical consumer is the dubious nature of much advertising. Parents teach their children, socialise them, to regard advertising with a degree of cynicism, and they have to do this in order to limit the demands placed on family budgets. Thus, with the assistance of handed on social wisdom, 'the main cultural effect of television advertising was to teach children that grown-ups told lies for money' (Heilbroner, 1976, p.90).

It is the very *activity* of social consumption which introduces some of the powerful difficulties that spring towards a quiescent labour market in this process. In short, active consumers choosing Turkey to holiday in rather than Spain, experience that activity in sharp contradiction to some supposed passivity within the world of work. The people who are encouraged to express 'choice' in the market experiences of consumption do so, and return to a world of work where their active interventions in the area of choice are decidedly *not* encouraged.

THE SOCIAL WORLD OUTSIDE OF WORK

Throughout the analysis of the four previous sectors we have stressed the way in which processes that are primarily seen as economic also contain an active social element. All of these social elements are experienced and constructed not simply in relation to various aspects of the world of work, but also collectively within the social world outside of work. Here consumption, reproduction, preparation for work, leisure and politics come together and in a temporal sense surround the experience of work. They surround it in age terms with young people and old people being excluded from the labour market. They surround it on a day by day basis with early mornings, late evenings and night, this for most workers being their time at home. In the week itself, for most workers it is the world of work that surrounds the weekend and the world of work that surrounds holidays.

This experience of *separation* between these two worlds is profound. Few people engage in paid labour in their homes and very few people live with their work. Since the world of work and the social world outside of work are experienced as profoundly different, their ideas, cultures and hopes can clash severely. Getting on at work can take place at the expense of home. The experience of women who are placed at the core of this contradiction by the gender inequalities of society demonstrate again and again in human terms the nature of the separation and differences between work and home. Trying to do both is to try and bring the rhythms and experiences of very different worlds together. The fit is far from easy either practically or ideologically. And it is this lack of 'fit' that is beginning to have such a significant effect on the labour market behaviour of so very many people.

LABOUR ACTIVITY: EXPLAINING THE DYNAMIC

Modern economies in the West are basically organised for commodity production in a money system, that is production occurs principally for the disposal of commodities through product markets in exchange for money. This has profound consequences which are transmitted by the action of competitive forces. One of the most important consequences is that businesses generally have to compete to make their products cheaper than their competitors and thus search for ways to raise their productivity. Those which fail to increase productivity end up with relatively expensive products and services and either clear them by reducing their profit margin or simply fail to sell them. Either way the more competitive firms eventually displace the less competitive.

The trend is, then, towards greater productivity because of the pressure of competition. In other words, simple circulation (leaving to one side production and marketing of raw materials and capital equipment) acts as a spur to productivity growth. The growth of productivity triggers further important consequences. The reduction of unit costs enables output to be expanded and the existing market to be expanded since more people can now exercise effective demand at the relatively lower price. However there are limits to the expansion of demand, and when markets become saturated businesses begin searching for new products. This may involve expenditure on research and development; it may involve the application of the latest scientific knowledge to the design of new products. Some firms specialise in finding and exploiting new product opportunities and become the creators of change in their industries (Miles and Snow, 1978, pp.55–7). Such businesses draw their top managers from management specialisms critical to their success, namely product development and marketing (ibid., p.60). The former needs no comment. Management specialists in the latter category, it should be noted, normally have an operational responsibility for the appropriateness and effectiveness of selling and for the expenditure on, and effectiveness of, promotional communications (Greenley, 1989, p.64). Selling and promotional communications of course relate to advertising, which plays a crucial role in the cultivation of consumer needs.

The discovery of new products can only be transformed successfully into new commodities if two conditions are met. Firstly, the producers have to find, stimulate or create new consumer needs to match these products; moreover these have to be needs which will materialise as effective demand – the consumers have to possess the money necessary to translate their need into effective demand within the market place.

Advertising is to the development of new needs amongst consumers as consumer credit is to the development of effective demand amongst would-be purchasers of commodities. Advertising and consumer credit are critical functions carried out by business organisations within simple circulation, essential for the cultivation of new product market conditions. As productivity continues to rise, there is a constantly renewed effort to find new products, and then to develop ever more elaborate and differentiated needs amongst consumers, using advertising and consumer credit.

The second condition for new products to be successfully turned into commodities is that the producers have to ensure that they have labour with the necessary skills and knowledge, and this tends to require the development of labour with qualitatively new aptitudes and competence.

The general conclusion is that the system of production based on the money system has an inherent, and self-sustaining, dynamic effect due to productivity growth, caused by competition between firms in simple circulation, with a concomitant need for business to find new avenues for investment. This is in no way negated by the fact that most new product ideas fail to make the grade as new commodities (Foxall, 1980, p.192). Nor does the fact that even products put on the market cannot always be guaranteed to sell as a result of advertising; consumer needs are not completely contingent on advertising, although advertising does have a powerful role in cultivating effective consumer demand.

The system of capitalist production, with simple circulation as a vital stage in the process, ensures consumer needs and labour skills and knowledge are constantly developing, widening and elaborating. The result – curse or boon depending on how it is perceived – is a restless and unceasing development of working lives and the way of life of the mass of people.

Understanding the dynamic nature of labour is historically contingent. In mature capitalist economies the social distribution processes become more important than in former phases of capitalist development. This is a result of two factors. Firstly, the capital accumulation process reaches a point where labour productivity grows primarily as a result of the application of fixed capital, especially in the form of automation. The general level of scientific and technical knowledge in society therefore becomes a critical factor. As a result, workers in advanced and successful economies are increasingly paid for their knowledge and understanding rather than their direct expenditure of energy. Secondly, the competition between capitalist firms has become more international in nature. This has repercussions for the relationship between business and the state. This relationship takes place within the paradigm of 'organised capitalism', which can take a variety of different forms and is not a simple contrast to laissez-faire capitalism. In general terms, it is clear that whereas organised capitalism is compatible with state regulation of simple circulation (state monopoly capitalism), manipulation of the money stock (monetarism), aggregate demand management (Keynesianism), organised capitalism at a mature phase has to involve state intervention in the reproduction of labour power. The explanation of this involves a distinction between two types of labour which are important for capital accumulation, one of which is productive labour, and the other which is a certain type of non-productive labour. As we have demonstrated it is this severely limited view of what actually is economic that dominates Thatcherism.

On strictly accounting grounds, the only type of activity which generates profit is that which produces goods and services which are marketed, that is, sold to buyers. Therefore workers in firms engaged in the production of marketed goods and services may be defined as productive from the point of view of being directly involved in work which is incorporated in commodities which are sold and realise a profit.

Teachers, trainers, medical workers, and others employed by the state in the provision of goods and services which are not marketed are formally non-productive. There is, since the goods and services are not sold, no realisation of a profit. There may of course be the result that consumers have important needs satisfied, but from an accounting point of view this is not the same as being involved in capital accumulation.

However where the effect of the work by, for example, state employed teachers is to raise the quality (skills and knowledge) of productive workers employed in capitalistic firms, and where the cost of the improvement in quality borne by the state is less than the increased profits due to gains in labour productivity, then state expenditure on 'free education' has become a part of the process of capital accumulation.

The reason for the state becoming involved in activity beneficial to capital accumulation can be understood negatively as the failure of capitalist entrepreneurial activity. Capital will only get involved in providing and forming the conditions of profitable production when to do so would be profitable. In the absence of opportunities for profitable activity, capitalist employers will leave it up to the state to create those conditions and will call on the state to fund the necessary expenditure through taxes. In the case of public education, we have an example of state services which are crucial for the creation of general conditions of capitalist production, these conditions being primarily concerned with increasing a major factor in the international competition based on labour productivity through scientific and technical know-how.

To sum up, social distribution is of major importance in raising the level of the forces of production in a country by providing the general social conditions for capitalist production, conditions which are necessary for successful international trading by capitalist firms, but which cannot be provided by productive labour (that is labour which results in marketed goods and services). The non-productive labour which is indirectly a source of capital accumulation has been termed second-order productive labour and it has been argued that it has had a major impact on the long-run record of capital accumulation (Habermas, 1974, pp.228–9).

The role of social distribution in the development of the quality of labour is obviously a factor of some importance in modifying and mediating the impulse originating from within simple circulation. The development of that modifying power of social distribution hinges critically on the degree to which workers develop a new relationship to their own self-development. Under laissez-faire capitalism, capitalist employers directed, changed, elaborated and complexified labour as a more differentiated phenomenon, in the search for new profitable avenues to invest capital released by the growing productiveness of labour. With the growth of the state's authority in the direction of the reproduction of labour power, it becomes possible for workers through their political parties to take part in the democratic process and thereby shape their own reproduction as labour power.

THE CONDITIONS OF THE DEVELOPMENT OF LABOUR

The conditions in which these processes take place can be very important in understanding the concrete experiences of particular countries at given times in their evolution. In this chapter we will just be noting what these conditions are, without following through their impact in a critical analysis of the development of labour.

There are six sets of conditions to which we will draw attention: (a) historical, (b) science and technology, (c) culture, (d) trade union organisation, (e) world markets and (f) social relations that surround production.

Historical

The historical conditions have been theorised by many different sociologists. Daniel Bell for example based his view of history on a triad of pre-industrial, industrial and post-industrial stages, corresponding to the successive dominance of agriculture, industry and services. It should be recognised that this understanding of historical conditions is based on the content of labour activity, and not on the form of social relationships characterising periods. Nor is it useful for understanding the immanent developments in the social relationships during specified periods. This is particularly important given the dynamic nature of labour which arises from processes based on the social relationships of capitalism, and which creates a shifting relationship between capital and labour even under capitalism. Nevertheless Bell's model has the virtue of recognising the pervasiveness of change and movement.

Another theoretical model of historical conditions has emphasised the rise of mass consumption society, based on a view of the Fordism era when advertising fostered uniform tastes amongst consumers as a necessary factor in the successful marketing of mass production goods. This isolated insight into the nature of contemporary society was useful in highlighting the importance of advertising. Galbraith's theory of the emergence of the 'technostructure' provides another example of the one-sided insight into contemporary economic processes. In this case the emphasis is placed on the administrative apparatus of big business organisations.

Goldthorpe and Lockwood's analysis of the development of a new or prototypical working class, based on the figure of an instrumental worker and his family engaged in privatised, home-centred consumption, reflects important developments in the living standards of workers and their families in advanced capitalism. But again their notion of the 'affluent worker' captures and highlights just one side of the interlinked developments which we have discussed above in connection with the five major processes. Producers, under the pressure of competition which triggers the growing productiveness of labour, are constantly seeking out new products and widening the circle of consumer needs and tastes, as the products themselves become relatively cheaper.

A comprehensive theorisation of historical conditions has to integrate all these one-sided insights and recognise them as reflecting an interlinked totality, in which the growth of science and technology, the increasing social productiveness of labour, the changing and elaborating pattern of marketed commodities, and the lifestyle of workers and their families are all interconnected. This was explicated in our discussion of the five basic processes above.

In particular, this one-sidedness of explanation mentioned above seems to search for a single economic dynamic to explain economic change. It is for example *caused* by technological innovation – or *caused* by the development of consumption patterns through advertising. Such a mono-causal view has some important repercussions with which we profoundly disagree.

Firstly, all such explanations are a-social. They do not involve the dynamics of organised social behaviour by groups of social members. Technology or advertisers make the history, and the people are made by that history. Peasants become workers because of a new machine. Their *activity* in the process is missing and consequently their activity in making history is missing. Under these circumstances, where history is made in a non-active way by forces beyond social relationships, it is possible to fashion the weirdest of historical explanations. One finds the powerful external force and wraps history and people's efforts around it.

Secondly, the contemporary *politics* of such explanations are profound. Since people are made by machines or advertisers, then what can people actually *do* about such things except sit around and wait for history to do them? Similarly if the *market* makes labour, and decides what is and what is not labour, then potential labour can achieve nothing by acting – it has to wait for whatever happens.

Thirdly, not only are these explanations undialectical in that they contain no social activity, but their very one-sidedness renders them occasionally absurd. Given for example the power of technology, how do we explain the extent to which a country, or a sector, does not involve itself with that technology. Those third world economies and peoples that do not must be judged 'backwards' because they do not use such technologies. Yet there are so many examples which demonstrate that when such technologies are used – in for example agriculture on the Saharan rim or beef production in Brazil – the consequences for the whole world are catastrophic. If the third world simply 'follows' modern technology down the CFC carbon route, then it is entirely possible that much of the world will cease to exist.

Science and technology

Science and technology has been incorporated into economic activity on a growing basis since the beginning of the industrial revolution. Nevertheless it is possible to identify 'spurts' in the quantitative development of this process. For example Hobsbawm sharply distinguishes the identities of British workers before and after the mid-20th century:

Technology introduced another and increasingly ominous distinction: unlike the nineteenth-century type of industry, which had an

almost unlimited demand for men and women without any
qualifications except strength and willingness, the technology of
the mid twentieth century has less and less use for them.... The
demand for skill increased sharply; not necessarily the flexible all-
round skill or adaptability of the nineteenth-century ideal – of
workers as well as administrative – but nevertheless high
specialization requiring a certain amount of training, intelligence,
and above all, prior formal education. Manual dexterity was no
longer enough. (Hobsbawm, 1969, pp.286–7)

Hand in hand with the changing requirements went, of course, the
development of social distribution, in the form of Britain's welfare
state.

One of the most obvious of social and political consequences of the
development of science and technology has been the differential social
methods of educating and training people and potential workers about
such advances. At every introduction of every technology developed
after the spinning jenny, there was a section of society that saw this
'machine' as replacing the use of labour in the productive process.
Every decade since then there has been stress upon the way in which
'work is finished' and therefore labour as an experienced activity is
both literally and historically redundant.

In contradistinction to such a view, another section of society has
realised the importance of developing the people and the workforce to
work with the machine through education and training. In two
different chapters we have highlighted the specific problems of English
capitalism's attempts to deal with this issue. But even despite these
failures there has been a recognition of the social necessity of such
organisation if the science and technology is to have any purchase on
the process of production.

Culture

The concept of culture can be difficult to pin down because it has been
very prone to a multitude of different usages. One of the most common
has seen it is as identical with the concept of style of life. Thus the
culture of the manual working class has been differentiated from that
of the white-collar working class. The differences in lifestyle are
themselves related to expenditure and consumption patterns; more
middle-class lifestyles necessitate more expenditure and qualitatively

different consumption behaviour. These differences are fragile, depending as they do on the occupational structure and this being, as we have seen earlier, constantly developed and 'complexified'. Their fragility also rests on the constant process of luxuries becoming necessaties for the various groups. Telephones, cars, overseas holidays, home computers, microwave ovens, etc. – the list of commodities which have made the journey, or are making the journey, from luxury to necessity is endless.

The culture of a group, or even a society, when we use culture as equivalent to lifestyle, has a dual relationship to the production process. This duality can be expressed as follows: culture sets limits on what can be successfully produced as commodities, and production seeks to drive beyond these limits through the use of advertising to change the culturally conditioned tastes of consumers.

Culture, even in this sense of a style of life, is more than just a bundle of consumer preferences for material commodities which are realised through simple circulation and social distribution. There are cultural interests which are are seen as important for the spiritual and 'cultural' development of the individual, with 'cultural' now referring to the artistic lifestyle of the individual. These are developed, especially in spare time, without the pressure of necessity from survival needs, although they do have connections with activity in the production process and in simple circulation. The spiritual and cultural development of individuals for example helps to form the personality structure of workers, and this may have profound repercussions on the experience of work: individuals may feel alienated from work which does not recognise their spiritual and cultural needs and they have to then force themselves to work consciously towards the end of production (that is the making of products and services).

Education plays an important part in the direct pursuit of cultural interests, which form the end purpose of a 'cultural' life style, as well as in the utilitarian development of a skilled and competent workforce. It therefore has a potential impact on the extent to which individuals feel gratified through work itself.

One factor which is most important in influencing a man's aspirations in the work process is education. The more education a person has received, the greater the need for control and creativity. For those with little education, the need for sheer activity (working to "keep occupied") and for association are more important than control, challenge, and creativity. (Blauner, 1964, p.29)

In view of this duality of education, it is of some significance that there has been an international trend in the 20th century to extend the full-time education process, with the result that the 'average' worker spends many more years in education than was once the case.

Trade union organisation

The role of collective bargaining by trade unions is most apparent in connection with simple circulation. The union role is not however confined to this process. The unions seek to make the 'investive' aspect of work as profitable as possible by maximising financial rewards for the energy expended in the production process. This affects both the scale of the effective demand emanating from employees and their families, and the rate of capital accumulation, which determines the upper limit of reinvestment (although credit may lead to this limit being exceeded). Trade unions also negotiate over the amount of energy expended in the production process, and this sets limits on the extent to which employers can pursue productivity rises through intensification of work. The more that unions rule out intensification, the more likely it is that employers will have to pursue productivity growth through exploitation of scientific and technological progress.

'Each country in the world has its own level of wages and working-class conditions, or indeed perhaps several different levels existing side by side for different sections of the population' (Cole, 1933, p.521). The level depends in part – but only in part – on the bargaining power of workers organised in trade unions. This in turn depends on the organisational unity of national trade union movements and on factors which mediate nominal and real wages, such as a country's internal price movements and the state's economic strategy for international trading.

World markets

Developments in the world economy, however abstract and remote they appear, have substantial importance for the processes we are examining. In the 19th century British workers were thought to be enjoying the fruits of an industrial monoply thoughout the world. 'The truth is this: during the period of England's industrial monopoly the English working-class have, to a large extent, shared in the benefits of the monopoly' (Engels, 1969, p.32). One implication of this is that world trading, and world markets, have an impact on simple circulation and on consumption. This impact can obviously work in different ways: in the 19th century workers in England enjoyed a higher standard of living than they would have otherwise done; at the same time, in order to gain this extra standard of living, the workforce of the Indian subcontinent had to suffer severe deprivation and hardship. The two were linked by colonialism and imperialism.

The role of market-led production was highlighted in Marx's comment that the Great Wall of China was battered down not by English cannon but by cheap shirts. Those shirts, it is true, were backed up by cannon, but acted as the front line of colonialism in that era.

The post-war experience of the 'loss of Empire' is not purely political. The role of Imperial preference in Empire markets was not a reciprocal one. English products were guaranteed a market niche in the third of the world coloured red on the map. As different colours change the map, so does different market penetration. England now has to compete in a different way with third world products, and the standard of living of the British citizen experienced a different effect from the world markets in the 1980s than it did in the 1880s.

Social relations that surround production

It is clear that the role of services in the reproduction of labour power is variable over time. In advanced capitalist countries the role of public services in the process of reproduction is enormous. This has politicised the social relations between labour and capital in a way that they were not under laissez-faire capitalism. Reproduction of labour-power by the state therefore has undermined the ability of those social relations to legitimise many different aspects of distribution and consumption in advanced society. There is a therefore tendency for the 'brakes' to be taken off the restraint of aspirations.

The growth of aspiration that springs from such publicly provided social conditions is not purely one of economic material production. It is also a *political* one. These political aspirations reflect the importance of the rights of workers to have a say in the way in which society is constructed. Having a say may then have further material effects – a problem which monetarist economists lament continually. In short, they end up profoundly worried about the extent to which democracy always provides greater public spending, which leads to greater political activity, which leads to greater public spending. Given this dynamic it is not surprising that Pinochet's Chile remained one of the main nations that has experimented most completely with monetarism.

These are some of the issues currently bound up in the current crisis conditions, which Offe has characterised as a crisis in crisis management by the state. Organised capitalism, which represented the state's attempt to overcome the disorganisation of unfettered capitalism, has turned into an unorganised–organised capitalism. The resolution of these *general* crisis conditions has led to attempts to return society to laissez-faire capitalism, which is fundamentally a project to dismantle social distribution. Alternative agendas to resolve the crisis exist, and thus enter into the development of the crisis conditions. One of these alternative agendas is to tackle the economic problems of mature capitalism while simultaneously reinvesting social relationships with a moral basis. This new moral basis is constructed from a synthesis of democratic values, gender and race equality, and a concern for the environment, adding up to a desire to pursue the 'good life'. (The specific, as opposed to the general, crisis conditions in publicly provided social conditions of production are the concern of the next chapter.)

CONCLUSIONS

Through their labour activity people transform themselves. Marx for example wrote:

> Labour is, in the first place, a process in which both man and Nature participate, and in which man of his own accord starts, regulates, and controls the material re-actions between himself and Nature. He opposes himself to Nature as one of her own forces, setting in motion arms and legs, heads and hands, the natural forces of his body, in order to appropriate Nature's productions in a form adapted to his own wants. By thus acting on the external world and changing it, he at the same time changes his own nature. He develops his slumbering powers and compels them to act in obedience to his sway. (Marx, 1974, p.173.)

Labour changes its nature by developing its physical and mental abilities and its slumbering powers, which is its general social productiveness, by progress in the scientific and technological world.

What we have seen in this chapter is that this result is produced essentially by a set of processes: production, simple circulation, political and social distribution, social consumption and processes in the social world outside of work. Paradoxically, maybe even confusingly, labour's movement towards a growth of its general social productiveness begins with expenditure and exhaustion of the capacity to labour in the production process; but this labour is not merely reproduced in the subsequent process of consumption, it is also of necessity developed as a result of simple circulation and through the process of political and social distribution. Without simple circulation and political and social distribution, the *growth* of labour's powers could not be realised.

9 An Assessment of the Cultural Conditions of Labour Today

INTRODUCTION

In the previous chapter we distinguished the processes which labour takes part in. These were production, simple circulation, political and social distribution, social consumption, and the whole network of social relations. Through these processes, people make things and consume them. Philosophically speaking they express themselves through their labour, indeed externalise themselves through their labour, and then their products return to them as objects of consumption, whether as products or services. This consumption takes place in the wider society.

We saw in the last chapter that the fact that labour has changed over the last two hundred years in Western capitalist economies, both in terms of workers' skills, competence, and capacity generally, and in terms of their needs as producers and the needs of them and their families as consumers, has to be due to the mediating processes of simple circulation and social distribution. This historical process is one of the main engines of social change.

Now, in this chapter, we have to recognise theoretically that these processes, from production through to consumption, are troubled by various imperfections and contradictions, and are disrupted in a multitude of ways in their actual operation in Britain today. The concrete situation we will be studying here comprises the period in Britain which began with the fuller construction of the welfare state by the Post-War Labour Government and which has encompassed the 'Restoration Period' of the 1980s when an attempt was made by the Thatcher administrations to revitalise market forces and the private sector. Some of these issues have been discussed earlier – here our task is one of summation.

The problems in these processes are studied stage by stage. We begin first with production, move on to look at simple circulation, then social distribution, and end by looking at consumption.

PRODUCTION

From the previous chapter we have seen that production in the money system of capitalism has in-built spurs to change in products and in the skills and competence of labour. But these changes do not occur smoothly, painlessly or perfectly. It is clear that they need social organisation and political intervention to make them happen.

As far as the changing skills, knowledge and competence of the workforce is concerned, one of the most important barriers to the development of new products is the inadequacy of British training. In Chapter 2 we have seen that the level and type of training in Britain is just not good enough. Workers with insufficient skills may be recruited, in which case their labour capacity has to be developed by the employer through on-the-job training or off-the-job training. When this training is make-shift, as it so often is, and when workers are left by a laissez-faire management to pick up new labour skills as best they can, the result is inefficiency. That means labour power is wasted and fails to realise its potential in terms of the products produced. Output is relatively low in quantity or poor in quality.

One form of crisis in the production process much debated in Britain is the operation of union organised restrictive practices. There is some credibility to the argument that restrictive practices are a response to inefficiency rather than a cause of it. The inefficiency in question is that of management, or so implies a view presented by Nichols.

The truth is of course that British trade unions have never been highly political nor, outside of some particular groups, highly militant...What British workers have been – or so it is commonly claimed – is less than fully cooperative. . . . A consideration of the sort of management that British workers have had to work with over several generations adds to its plausibility. . . . Workers whose experience leads them to think that 'management doesn't know what it's doing' may be less than keen to make good for management what they think management should have done already, etc., etc. (Nichols, 1986, p.218)

A quite different problem occurs when we consider the consumptive element of production (Offe, 1984). The design of work in Britain has not kept pace with workers' needs for humanised working conditions. The poor quality of working life is experienced as such by British workers. Chapter 7 reviewed some of the evidence and we saw that British workers are more alienated than workers in other countries. The effects of this show up as job dissatisfaction and lack of workforce commitment, and ultimately in productivity problems and turnover problems.

SIMPLE CIRCULATION

Simple circulation is in crisis in a number of different ways. Firstly, there is the issue of labour shortages which effect different parts of the labour market at different times. These differences are both geographical and sectoral. In the 1950s there were chronic skill shortages and also large-scale destruction of local industries, such as the Durham coal field. Some of the labour moved from Durham to Nottinghamshire coalfields and some people stayed in the ex-pit villages and stopped being labour.

Whilst such labour shortages may appear obvious for the 1950s, the continuance of different labour shortages when there were three million unemployed in either the 1930s or the 1980s needs more explanation. In terms of skill shortages, the immediate answer is that individual firms experience shortages because they will not pay the rate necessary to attract the labour required. But then there is one of the most intractable problems: the reluctance of businesses to train people because they fear that trained employees will move on to other employers.

Secondly, simple circulation is also in crisis in respect of the purchase of commodities. In the late 1980s it took the particular form of consumption without production due to the mediating role of consumer credit. Marcus Fox, a Conservative MP, defended the Government's increase of interest rates to 15 per cent in October 1989. When interviewed on BBC's Radio 4, he accused the British people of treating money as if it had no value. This is either a meaningless statement – or one of great perspicacity. It is meaningless if you regard money as merely the medium of circulation – it has no intrinsic value –

its sole purpose is to facilitate buying and selling. On the other hand, if money represents objectified labour, congealed labour, then money has a value based on the socially necessary labour incorporated in the products resulting from production. Consumer credit provides people with the ability to purchase commodities in advance of, or even instead of, obtaining money in the form of wages. If the credit is obtained and used in disregard of the earning capacity and costs of living of individuals and their families, then the acts of purchase lose a relationship to what is being earnt by taking part in production. Money therefore no longer represents congealed labour – it is simply a medium of exchange. And the only limit on what is purchased is the amount of credit that credit institutions are prepared to make available – production no longer acts as a limit on what is purchased and consumed.

Credit therefore becomes the obvious and powerful method through which consumption is increased without any increase in earning power. Apparently it provides an almost limitless capacity to keep the sphere of circulation actually going round.

The havoc that this can create in the disproportion between producing and consuming was fully revealed by the ex-Chancellor of the Exchequer Nigel Lawson in early November 1989. In a television interview he was accused of making a mess out of the British economy by going for growth through tax cuts. Lawson denied this and insisted that the Conservative Govenment had maintained a tight discipline over the money supply (using the narrow measure of money M0 to monitor the growth of the money supply) and had maintained fiscal discipline. The problem, he said, was not the tax cuts. The problem was that 'freeing up' the system had led to a growth of borrowing. Whereas tax cuts in Spring 1988 had put 4 billion pounds sterling into the economy, he reckoned that borrowing had put 40 billion pounds into it.

The growth of borrowing, and the less observed decline of personal saving in the 1980s, represented a massive growth of effective demand. It was increasingly apparent in the late 1980s that the system, now it had been 'freed', was not necessarily able to match the boost to demand by a boost to the supply of goods and services by UK firms. Official figures showed rising inflation and a balance of payments deficit on the current account, indicating that supply was not rising adequately to cover the increased demand and that the growth of supply was disproportionately resulting from imports.

Table 4 The consumer boom and its correlates in the United
Kingdom 1985–89

	Per cent increase on last year				
	1985	1986	1987	1988	1989
(a) Consumers' expenditure	3.7	5.7	6.0	7.0	3.8
(b) Personal saving ratio	9.5	8.2	5.7	4.1	5.0
(c) Inflation (RPI)	6.1	3.4	4.2	4.9	7.8
(d) Imports of goods and services	2.5	6.8	7.6	12.6	7.1

Source: _Economic Progress Report_ (Treasury) No.207, April 1990, p.8.
Note: The personal saving ratio is personal saving as a percentage
of personal disposable income.

The implication of Lawson's defence of the Government's financial
strategy was that the economic problems in the late 1980s were due to
developments in simple circulation and were not due to social
distribution. As he explained, tax and public spending was not a
problem – excessive consumer spending power due to borrowing was.
  The cultural significance of these developments is a contradictory
one for labour. The expansion of consumer credit permitted expansion
of consumption without production, purchasing without earning. The
result was that aspirations and desires of consumers were not held back
or placed under self-restraint and labour became conscious of itself as
consumer with needs and aspirations. If this expansion of consumer
credit fostered the consciousness of labour as consumer, it also,
because of the failure of production to respond to increased effective
demand, led to a declining self-consciousness of labour as producer. In
a real sense, money lost its value as far as value had to be linked to day
by day earning.
  The national statistics showed instead the growing power of overseas
producers in Japan, Korea, Germany and elsewhere who were making
the products that British consumers wanted. Its effect was to reinforce
the feeling of demoralisation which accompanies the growing
consciousness that a nation is dependent on others: they (people in
other countries) had become independent as we had become
dependent. The satisfaction of our needs rested on their production.
The feeling that 'something' is wrong mounts with the deteriorating
balance of payments.

Table 5   United Kingdom's balance of payments 1985–9

Year	Current account (pounds, billions)
1985	3.16
1986	- 0.04
1987	- 4.4
1988	-15.02
1989	-20.85

Source: *Economic Progress Report* (Treasury) No.207, April 1990, p.4.

Since money lost its close relationship with what was earnt, it was inevitable that such a process would create great *social* difficulties. The result is that labour gained in its feeling that it existed as consumer and diminished in its feeling that it existed as producer. In consequence the gains in the standard of living were attended by a feeling that they were not permanent or real gains. They could fade away.

Consumer booms may be choked off by high interest rates. But the subsequent choking of consumption by high interest rates cannot simply restore the situation to what it was before. Aspirations will persist as the negative experience of frustrated self-gratification. More importantly, the ability of the Government to deal with inflation and the massive balance of payments problem was never in doubt (even if some wondered whether they had the will to manage them). What was in doubt was the ability of the Government to tackle the underlying or root causes of the economy's problems.

Any judgement on this matter has to put the economic crises of the late 1980s into the longer historical perspective of the series of post-war crises in the British economy. Starting with the Conservative administrations of the 1950s we had an attempt to free up the system by dismantling the state controls on the economy. Shonfield describes the outstanding feature of the 1950s as being 'a kind of vigorous back-pedalling, the expression of a nostalgia for some bygone age when market forces produced the important economic decisions, while governments merely registered them' (Shonfield, 1965, p.99). Thirty years later there was another balance of payments crisis and interest rates were again the preferred remedy. Circulation rather than production was again being dealt with.

The early 1960s saw a swing away from worship of the market: state intervention was back in favour. This decade saw the British state take the route of social democracy: the state could correct the imperfections in market forces. The Wilson Government of the 1960s launched a modernisation strategy aimed at getting the economy in shape. To some degree this meant modifying simple circulation; for example incomes policies regulated pay rises given to employees. To some extent it meant supplementing the efforts of the private sector; the massive growth and experimentation in public sector education, for instance, was inaugurated in a spirit of scientific and technological confidence.

So the developments in the 1980s represented a return to the national economic strategy of the 1950s – and led to a return of the problems of that decade, notably the excessive claims on simple circulation (consumer demand in excess of domestic supply of goods and services). If simple circulation can support this crisis of expectations it means that the discipline of the market is a fiction. Where else can the state turn for its solution if not the market? Does this mean that state determined high interest rates have to be used to re-socialise the general public because the market has no self-discipline? Has the failure of the late 1980s shown clearly that simple circulation cannot be left to private persons, and that the state has to set the cultural norms of consumers if simple circulation is not to degenerate into the ill-disciplined anarchy of market forces?

Social democracy attempted to influence simple circulation through a series of different sorts of incomes policies. These, either backed up by law or social compact between Government and unions, were direct attempts to intervene in the amount which was allowed to circulate and the manner in which it happened. In a very simple sense there was an attempt to create a 'norm' of what should be circulated and then to enforce that norm. There were two main difficulties in this approach.

Firstly, there was very little else in the way of cultural norms being promulgated. Society as a whole outside of the realm of circulation remained at the mercy of the market mechanism, with very little thought of intervention or regulation of behaviour. Even in other areas of circulation there was no regulation. This created a distinct impression of 'unfairness'.

Secondly, the intervention in the sphere of circulation did little to directly affect the sphere of production. Only limited interventions took place in that sphere when they happened at all. Consequently the basic issue of improvements in production were not dealt with.

The market-led approach of the 1950s and 80s fares little better. Here the belief is that the market will discipline the sphere of circulation. This discipline, as with incomes policy, is based on only some sections of circulation. The market is allowed to find its own level in all but the sphere of pay. Here, apart from several years of mass unemployment, the concept of 'high' pay awards demonstrates that a market-led approach to the settlement of pay does not lead to a neutral approach. Politically there are exhortations to lower or change the nature of the market outcomes.

Of greater importance though, is the failure to deal with the sphere of circulation in terms of credit. A *growth* in one year of 40 billion pounds of consumer credit, when compared to a *total* education expenditure in that one year of 19 billion demonstrates the power of that sort of surge in circulation. Again it has no direct effect upon the sphere of production, since such an increase in demand can be met quite simply by an increase in imports, bypassing British production completely.

SOCIAL DISTRIBUTION

Social distribution expanded considerably in two periods of growth after the second world war, and then the state, under Thatcherism, set about limiting it. The political background to Thatcherism's assault on social distribution was the crisis in social democracy. This came to a head in the 1970s, which had to contend with shock to the world markets due to oil price rises, and during which the theory of ungovernability was gaining ground. The 'winter of discontent' in 1978–9 raised to a fever pitch the debate over the ungovernability of Britain according to the principles of social democracy, and heralded the advent of Thatcherism. It was not only in Britain that the issue of ungovernability raged (Offe, 1984), but perhaps nowhere else was this issue resolved so decisively in favour of the 'New Right'.

The 'New Right' alleged that the welfare state had become overburdened with expectations and a growing proportion of national income was being drawn into the public sector by means of taxation. Keith Joseph claimed that two world wars were to blame: 'Wars create great expectations and the belief that government can do almost anything' (Joseph, 1978, p.100). The New Right were particularly concerned that the welfare state led people to perceive they had 'rights' which they did not have. Keith Joseph expressed the New Right's view on this matter in fairly succinct terms:

The mood of this time was one of guaranteeing rights, which really amounted to claims. But in any society, the sums of rights (and claims) must equal the sum of duties. When government promises more in the way of rights than it is willing or able to impose as duties, one has inflation of rights. In a money economy, this leads to inflation of the currency. Governments – and others who can – try to circumvent money, creating additional non-monetary rights, which of course lead to monetary inflation. (Keith Joseph, 1978, p.101)

This not only set the main economic priority as the fight against inflation, it also indicated the New Right's belief in the existence of a crisis in democracy under the welfare state: the politicians were busy promising rights in line with the Utopian expectations of a population socialised by the experiences of wartime conditions. The New Right needed a new style of politician, one who ruled by conviction, and who believed in being cruel to be kind. No more acting according to social compassion, since this was at the tax payer's expense, and led to economic ruin. Above all it implied the need for Government to cut back on the 'burden' of the state sector, as this was how the inflation of rights was being manifested.

In the 1970s there was a particularly acute panic over the public sector share of national income – this came to a head during the period of the social contract. The New Right and others attacked the public sector as draining the life-blood of the private sector, making the latter unnaturally feeble, and they attacked the welfare state as being too expensive. They began to debate the quantitative limits of the public sector: 'Even 40 per cent is very high, perhaps too high, when it means that the private sector is milked in order to support increasing legions of deficitary activities' (Joseph, 1978, p.102).

In essence the New Right's solution was to reduce social distribution and to cut down on state regulation of the private sector and of simple circulation. The favourite terms of this New Right's language was deregulation and privatisation.

Thatcherism represented the New Right in political power. Initially the Thatcher administration saw its task as a quantitative and a qualitative limitation of social distribution, necessary to liberate the private sector. The rationale for quantitative limitation was based on the Thatcher state's non-recognition of the public sector economy. The economy was seen as essentially the private sector economy and this was presumed to have its own spontaneous dynamism. The public sector economy was not seen – or not recognised – as a proper part of the economy and the private part was represented as the whole. The dynamism of the private sector was seen as nullified by the dead weight of the public sector, which was perceived as having no dynamic role to play in the economy. It simply drained off wealth through the need for high taxation to pay for it.

The rationale for the qualitative limitation of the public sector was partly based on the view that the private sector was choked and inhibited by state regulations. More fundamentally, the New Right believed that the economy (meaning the private sector part of it) could only pursue its own logic and potential if the state's crisis handling activities were suppressed. This was the sense in which they wanted a qualitative limitation of social distribution.

The New Right did recognise the economy as being in a deep crisis, one that consisted fundamentally of an excess of demands over the wealth creation capacity of the economy. Its solution to the crisis was primarily a change of state strategy to suppress the state's own crisis suppressing activities, in order that the market's own crisis resolving capacity could be freed.

The state under Thatcherism defined its role as being to create the framework for wealth creation by the private sector. In line with the identified need to limit social distribution both quantitatively and qualitatively, this framework was ideally posited as consisting of three elements: monetary discipline, fiscal discipline (cutting back spending by the public sector) and an enterprise culture. In 1983 this strategic view of the content of the framework was expressed by Nigel Lawson, the Chancellor of the Exchequer, when speaking at the Lord Mayor's banquet for merchants and bankers of the City of London. He told his City of London audience that the Government would continue downward pressure on public sector borrowing and that this would require strict control of Government spending. He said there would be no relaxation of the fight against inflation:

> The rules by which we have operated policy have been an unequivocal guide to expectations. They have set the framework within which decisions are made. The rules are clear but must necessarily be interpreted with discretion. Our objective...is to achieve sustainable non-inflationary growth.
>
> The twin pillars of our policy remain the Medium Term Financial Strategy and the encouragement of enterprise in the market-place. (Treasury, 1983, p.2)

The first two parts of the framework – monetary and fiscal discipline – were to be installed immediately by the Thatcher Government; the cultural change was to be accomplished in due course. The result in actuality is that social distribution became racked by a variety of essentially political crises.

For, whilst the Government collected three mandates in 1979, 1983 and 1987 for the diminution of the public sector and its expenditure, there were severe political and material repercussions in engaging in cuts in public expenditure in many areas. There may have been a general agreement with the belief that public expenditure was 'too high', but actually making cuts creates real problems in each specific issue. In the health service and in social security, public expenditure has continued to increase throughout the Thatcher years. For most of that period the Government made a virtue out of cutting expenditure in these areas, but actually found it necessary to increase that expenditure. The specific issue of political opinion has demonstrated that it is not possible to cut health spending or social security.

Interestingly though, by the end of the 1980s there was a public impression that certain services had been cut by a ruthless Government. This impression, when allied to the fact that in some areas such as housing and higher education there had been real cuts in expenditure, led to a cultural reaction which has social and economic ramifications. It led to a situation in which people became more atomised in their social attitudes. Although Thatcherism endorsed this atomisation – it was said that there was no such thing as 'society' – it weakened a key source of work motivation. People could not be asked to work harder, or better, for 'society' . Working harder or better had to be grounded in self-interest instead.

The policies of monetary and fiscal discipline pursued by the Government also had material outcomes that interfered with smooth production. So by the end of 1988, the CBI estimated, the lack of investment in infrastructure in London was costing business 15 billion pounds a year. This was a sum considerably higher than the tax cuts which a lack of public expenditure was meant to have created.

The Thatcher Government also experienced a crisis in its strategy for handling the overall crisis of the economy. This took two forms. Firstly, its dogmatic faith in the market had led it to make changes which did not work. These changes centred on a dual strategy of forcible state-instigated commodification of labour and the use of passive revolution to engineer private sector entrepreneurial hegemony. Both these require further analysis.

The state attempts to force people to enter the labour market by very distinctive patterns of intervention in the sphere of distribution. Very specific changes to the way in which people can claim benefit when unemployed have been designed to force people onto the labour market – to accept any job when they would previously have chosen to wait for an offer of work to arise.

The training schemes for both youth (YTS) and older people (ET) have also been shown to have very little to do with training. In 1989, when unemployment was declining, the Government diminished their training budget. It was at this time that all commentators were claiming that the country needed more training; but the Government expenditure in this area had only taken place in a direct relationship to unemployment. Once that diminished, then so did the training budget.

A passive revolution organised by the state on behalf of private sector entrepreneurs was initially announced by Thatcherism in the phrase that Government would create the framework for economic success. Implicit in this notion of the state as responsible for the framework was the counter-notion that some other group was to be responsible for the content of activity within the framework. The Thatcher Governments had cast private sector business leaders for this starring role.

The crisis in this respect comes down to its fetishism of market forces. It looked on capital as having freedom in an absolute sense because the Government had deregulated and privatised, but overlooked the fact that freedom cannot ignore necessity. The necessity for capital is to purchase labour power and sell commodities at a profit. Take, for example, the unleashing of private initiative to deal with the problem of insufficient training. This initiative has to confront barriers created by necessity – created, in fact, by the market. If capital simply trains labour power but does not enjoy the benefit of that training because the labour power has moved on to competitors, capital, or rather the individual capitalist, is in danger of not realising profit. In Britain this fear is greatly enhanced because of the lack of state support for training and the laissez-faire and casual attitudes of employers towards hiring and firing labour.

This fetishism problem was even greater where the state wanted employers to get involved in funding education. The City Technology Colleges were, for example, in the end an experiment which was only saved by expanding the public sector contribution.

As noted above, Thatcherism's longer term aim with regard to the framework was to change psychological and social factors in the

British situation – known as a whole as bringing about 'an enterprise culture'. This aim is also in crisis. Keith Joseph identified long ago the need to change attitudes: 'The last thing we should do is join the social engineers in giving the impression that the economy is simply a vast mechanical system in which, if the right levers are pulled, the right results must come up' (Joseph, 1978, p.99). At its crudest they wanted people to see work as the place where money had to be made before it could be spent. And they wanted families to take care of themselves rather than rely on the welfare state.

This demonstrates some important relationships being developed within the labour market that, we believe, have severe implications for the way in which that market has become unravelled in the late 1980s. Firstly, the enterprise culture says people are meant to go out and sell new ideas, take risks and build up markets. None of this has any real purchase on the lives of nearly every person in the labour force in the country.

It is true that the self-employed sector may have increased over this period, but it has never been claimed that everyone can become a small employer. *Most* people will remain as workers and the enterprise culture purely gives them – the majority – a supporting role to the stars who are building the new markets. They can feel grateful that others are engaged in that culture but have no role – apart from moderating their wage demands – in its construction.

The second issue is the link between work being the place where money was made in order to consume in the bosom of ones' family. This was a severe underlining of the way in which work should be seen as a means to an end. One goes there only to earn money to spend elsewhere. Firstly, this must lead to a struggle for wage increases – since if you get paid lots of money for doing very little you are succeeding in that culture. Secondly, it will also mean that the experience of work is purely instrumental. As a means to an end, one's life will be made elsewhere. If there is any way possible of getting that end without the means – by capitalising a housing investment for example – people will do that. Work for itself becomes much less important and entry, or re-entry, into the labour market has less social significance for people.

Bringing in an enterprise culture was not seen as filling a vacuum. This culture had to be brought in by extinguishing an anti-enterprise culture. The New Right blamed education for the socialisation of Britain's young people in anti-business attitudes. They also blamed it for an anti-business snobbery which diverted the best of the young people into the civil service, into the professions, into university life, in fact, into anything but business careers. Public education was suspect and had to be changed. The anti-enterprise culture of schools would be transformed into the 'enterprise culture'.

The crises in Thatcherism's attempt to deal with crises in the state, have led to important developments which represent attempts to respond to the failures experienced. The most important of these come under two broad headings: firstly, the passive revolution is passing over into an attempt by the state to overcome market forces, and secondly, the attempt to restructure education for business is turning into an attempt to educate business!

The transformation of passive revolution into state abolition of free competition and market forces is expressed most powerfully in the initiative to set up Training and Enterprise Councils (TECs). The proposals on TECs were set out in the White Paper *Employment for the 1990s*. This should perhaps have been entitled 'Employers for the 1990s' since the end is really to make employers in a new image. It was not intended for trade unionists – it was plain that the Government contemplated with equanimity no role at all for trade unions if they did not adapt. It was take it or leave it as far as the unions were concerned.

The TECs are to be small groups consisting mainly of top private sector executives, plus a minority of others, who are to supervise and direct the spending of public funds on training in localities. This activity was formerly carried out by the MSC. The proposal is clearly meant to get individual local capitals accustomed firstly to working together, and secondly to spending money on training. Perhaps the Government hopes that these habits will become sufficiently established for the activity to become generalised and self-sustaining. They clearly imagine they are dealing with mental muscles that have become atrophied through non-use.

The major contradiction in the White paper is that the key institutional innovation is a negation of competition, and this from a Government *for* the free market! The Government hopes to use public money and the TECs to re-educate Britain's private employers into being responsible in the development of labour. Either they are asking private employers to do something which is against their traditional nature in Britain, or they are trying to make the private sector better by organising training without free competition. The chances of this being a short term educational phase which results in the full introduction of a private sector based training system cannot be discounted, but they look relatively small.

The failure of education to restructure has had a peculiar history to it in the 1980s, in which the credit for attempts to restucture are awarded to teachers and the blame is heaped on business people. Schools, despite resource constraints and teacher shortages, respond with secondments, work shadowing, work experience, the search for sponsorship and business links; and business responds with nothing. This failure is proclaimed most of all by business leaders, who say the target is now business.

Politically the end of this first phase is signalled by the winding up of Industry Matters, a vehicle designed to re-educate education as to the importance of industry. It ends with the realisation that education has responded but that few employers have become involved. Industry Matters had become 'dominated' by education: the few employers involved being continuously embarrassed by the disproportion in the numbers of educationalists attending meetings, events and conferences. Indeed, DTI and Training Agency civil servants, BIC and Industry Matters quasi-civil servants, seconded managers, management consultants, enterprise agency staff and others operating at least one step removed from business, make up a vast army of officials facilitating education-industry links; these are the second largest group after the teachers in this activity to mediate education and industry. The odd 'men' out in these gatherings are the real business entrepreneurs!

Also, the blame on schools for setting unreal expectations in the minds of young people with regard to their attitudes to work is turning into exhortation to employers to build commitment through employee involvement.

The response to the crisis in their stategy for dealing with the economic crisis, is producing a third level of crisis. This is the crisis of support amongst its own supporters. Not least is the problem that their supporters cannot keep up with the profusion and rapid succession of government initiatives.

The inherent contradiction of Thatcherism was that it tried to free the private sector from the state by *abolishing* social distribution. Freedom for the private sector was not capable of realisation in this way. Firstly, the private sector needs social distribution in order to realise its wealth-creating role, and doing away with the public sector and social distribution merely throws the private sector into chaos. Secondly, the realisation of a thriving private sector rests on the self-awareness and self-confidence of entrepreneurs, whereas the enterprise culture has been aimed primarily at socialising workers and their families. In addition, freeing the private sector was also flawed by the contradiction that the state's interventions were oriented to freeing finance capital even to the extent that it left productive capital without the necessary conditions to engage in wealth creating activity.

The theoretical flaw in Thatcherism was manifested in the New Right's conclusion that inflation was Government made. This was proved, at the end of 10 years of Thatcherism, to be wrong. As Nigel Lawson said, the Government had controlled monetary and fiscal policy, but private borrowing by consumers had created inflationary problems. Higher interest rates were to be the cure – but make no mistake, this was a state solution to a problem which was in his opinion not of Government's making. The Thatcherites had hoped to put an end once and for all to the problems of contradictions between making money and spending it, between effort and reward. These contradictions they had diagnosed as due to Government's attempting to meet excessive expectations. They said that these illusory expectations could only be met, falsely, by actions which resulted in the Government making inflation.

Why did they make the theoretical error of seeing the Government as the only producer of inflation? The answer is fundamentally because they saw social distribution in a one-sided way: goods and services paid for by the state on the basis of revenue collected from the private sector and by state borrowing. The role of social distribution in the realisation of the development of labour was ignored or devalued. It has been said, with reference to the Thatcherite slogan that people should 'get on their bikes' to look for work, that the bike is in fact education and training. And of course, education and training are very often provided under social distribution.

The one-sidedness of their view of social distribution stemmed from the fact that they had been blinded by the immediate appearance of the economy as concerned with the making of money. The correctness of their emphasis on Britain's economic activities being based on a money economy was contradicted by their failure to recognise that the essence of such an economy rested on production of goods and services by labour. In the end they paid the price of fetishising money relations and devaluing labour.

The lack of a role for labour in this plot, except as a simple hard working support for business and the family, inevitably means that labour is not valued. Making money out of any other sort of activity is valued highly. Under these circumstances people can make money much more easily through credit and simultaneously with the making of that money decrease the social value of their own labour. The long term implications of this for a nation which needs labour to produce are catastrophic. Perhaps there was real belief that it was possible to construct an economy based totally upon an international rentier principle – but if so, the role of labour as simple parasite upon the rentier has also not been politically or socially explained.

CONSUMPTION

Employers want to recruit young people who have some capacity for development into capable and effective staff. One manager from a retail multiple in London told us that they found such people difficult to find. They had to have the right attitude and they had have to 'something' already – something that the managers could work on and develop. They looked for the presence of this ill-defined something in the leisure activities of the job applicants – did they have interests and hobbies?

People who spend all their time watching television or doing nothing, or who have very little sign of energy, are not what today's employers are looking for. But passive consumerism is precisely what business has been busy cultivating for years. Package holidays where it is all laid on, sitting in front of the 'telly', *watching* football (which the authorities are trying to turn back into a passive spectator sport) are all passive. Watching television is *the* great leisure 'activity' of the late 20th century – the past-time (or is it pass-time) for kids and grown-ups which takes a day a week (one-seventh of life). Watching television turns from entertainment, to education, to 'doing nothing' as imperceptibly as an eye-blink. And it turns from one to the other without any need for any external visible movement from the 'watcher' at all. The passivity of television consumption is shown by the way that the nature of the activity (entertainment, education, or 'doing nothing') is unobservable. We can only know what the activity is by asking the watcher.

Passive consumerism has been cultivated. It was not fashioned out of nothing. There had to be 'something' there for business marketing and advertising to work on. It had to have a base in the consumer's make-up that could be developed. But it was cultivated. And now employers complain because young people are too often devoid of 'external' visible signs of liveliness – at least of a sort they feel they can harness. Too many of them strike the employers as lacking passion, drive and commitment. The one youngster who comes along with get up and go, with commitment and activity to put into the job, are seen as the exception.

The contradictions around consumerism and activity are many. Whilst employers stress the importance of a self-directed activity amongst their potential workers, they only mean that to happen within very strict cultural guidelines. They want a workforce to be active but respectful.

In the context of how young people express their self-actualization within youth culture, this is entirely the opposite of what employers want. For the greatest amount of youth culture in its mass and passive form only allows certain sorts of activity to emerge *against* this passivity. Thus young people can go to concerts providing they sit and listen or scream in the right places. If they act differently from that they have to construct their own activity *against* certain other forms of regulation. Young people are meant to engage in sexual activities only in a set of soft fantasies prescribed by Australian soap operas. These are passive. When they construct their sexual activity it is done against this softness, and often in the ignorance that leads to pregnancy. The same is true for going on holiday (lager louts), watching football (hooligans) and constructing their own modes of dressing (wierdos). The alternative to hooligans, louts, sluts and wierdos are passive boring teenagers whom the employers do not seem to want.

THE REALISATION OF LABOUR IN SOCIAL RELATIONS

There is such a thing as society. These apparent economic processes actually occur in specific social relations. Our analysis highlights this specificity.

The state under Thatcherism gave up a lot. It gave up promising full employment. It gave up promising to meet people's expectations. It gave up promising security to those who worked in the public sector. But it also aimed high. It aimed to provide the right monetary and fiscal framework for growth. It aimed to restore attitudes of thrift and a willingness by workers to be mobile ('on your bike'). And it aimed to break restrictive practices and restore incentives for enterprise.

In a money economy (to use Keith Joseph's term), competitiveness is the crucial factor in trading performance. Economies which are uncompetitive eventually succumb to those that are competitive. The competitiveness of an economy can be measured in various ways, but one of the most commonly used indicators is unit labour costs. Other things being equal, unit labour costs go up because labour costs are rising and go down because the productiveness of labour is rising. The

table below shows that the UK's competitive position deteriorated
markedly by comparison to the leading capitalist economies in the
1970s. It also shows, however, that between 1979 and 1988, the period
of Thatcherism, it was still deteriorating markedly by comparison,
especially with Japan.

Table 6   Index of unit labour costs 1970–88

Year	UK	US	Japan	W. German
1970	100	100	100	100
1971	109	102	112	110
1972	116	102	117	114
1973	121	105	123	122
1974	144	116	158	136
1975	186	129	192	146
1976	206	133	192	144
1977	223	138	200	149
1978	253	147	196	156
1979	291	157	190	158
1980	356	172	192	170
1981	389	185	200	178
1982	408	198	215	181
1983	414	191	217	181
1984	428	188	206	181
1985	450	191	210	181
1986	473	191	217	188
1987	477	190	212	195
1988	491	191	–	192

Source: Calculated from OECD, *Main Economic Indicators*, various
            issues.

Why was the UK's competitive position deteriorating? Part of the
explanation was that wage costs rose much more in the UK than in the
other three countries. (Labour costs include wages, but they include
other costs as well.) But then again they needed to, since price rises over
the period of Thatcherism have been much greater than in Japan and
West Germany, and even than in the United States which did not fare
as well as the other two. In fact 'British workers' wages remain low by
international standards' (Nichols, 1986, p.219).

There was evidence that the trends in labour costs were seen as a productivity issue by manufacturers' leaders in Britain. According to Nichols,

> The alarm bells were sounding about British unit labour costs as early as April 1984, when CBI Director-General Sir Terence Becket took the unusual step of urging chief executives to adopt a unit labour cost target.... Speaking in Liverpool, he referred to a looming 'productivity crisis'. (Ibid., 1986, p.220)

It also seems to have been the case that the effects of the deteriorating unit labour costs were delayed by the fall in the value of the pound. In late 1984 the Bank of England 'drew attention to an important factor that has helped to obscure the true extent of the problem that British manufacturing industry continues to experience with productivity – that "UK manufacturing industry would have steadily lost cost competitiveness over the past year had it not been for the decline in sterling's effective rate"' (*ibid.*, 1986, p.221). Treasury figures showed the Sterling Exchange Rate Index was falling from 1980 to 1987.

Table 7 Sterling exchange rate index (1975 = 100)

Year	Index
1979	87.3
1980	96.1
1981	95.3
1982	90.7
1983	83.3
1984	78.6
1985	78.3
1986	72.8
1987	72.7
1988	76.5

Source: Treasury, *Economic Progress Reports*, Nos 172, 181, 187, 193, 197, and 200.

So a pretty massive fall in sterling coincided with deteriorating unit labour costs for much of the 1980s. If sterling had not declined, Britain's international competitiveness would have been bleak indeed.

The fact is that Thatcherism continued to emphasise the importance of flexibility in working practices and labour mobility as important sources of productivity growth. It is noticeable that this places the onus on labour to intensify its contribution to the production process and to achieve greater returns from capital without any necessary productivity gains from the use of fixed capital, or from enhancing the quality and productiveness of labour through education or training. It is a state labour strategy of squeezing more out of a system through the initiative of labour without any change in the system's basic parameters.

Closing the gap with West Germany and Japan would have taken a different state strategy for greater productiveness of labour. We are left wondering how much greater productiveness could have been achieved by using social distribution properly, for example by adequate and targetted public funding of education and training. And could more have been done earlier by the state to encourage greater investment in training by employers?

ROOT CAUSES

Many but not all of the problems found in the concrete operation of the various processes considered can be traced back to the lack of value placed on labour in Britain. This simple fact has deep and profound implications for all aspects of economic life and leads to a multitude of crises phenomenon. Where does it come from – this lack of value placed on labour?

It is part of a syndrome in Britain. It's one expression of a pathology which can be observed in all aspects of economic life under the hegemony of private capitalism. And the state has at times, although not consistently and only belatedly under the Thatcher administrations, been engaged in a process of teaching capital to value labour. As the 1980s drew to a close, the Conservative Government recovered the post-war concern for the valuing of labour. This was shown by the attempt to create employer-led bodies to establish training, and the commissioning of research to foster employee involvement. The importance of well-trained and committed labour power was officially proclaimed.

But this can only be seen as an attempt, one that is compromised and confused by its association with New Right Government, to overcome a crisis in British capitalism. Its existence shows the gap between the notion of well-trained and highly committed workers and the objective situation. The assessment has to be that things look bad judged in terms of the idea of a modern, skilled and motivated workforce.

The overall pathology of British capitalism rests on one simple fact. The means have turned into an end. The basic ground for successful international trading is production. Production not just of physical goods but also services. Financial systems are a means to successful production. Financial activity comes out of production activity. No matter how much financial activity develops and elaborates, it is nothing if it does not return to its basis in production. Efficient, cost-effective systems of financial activity are crucial for maximising wealth creation.

But where financial activity becomes an end rather than merely a means, a pathological situation has arrived. When finance is seen as important and production (not just manufacturing) is seen as unimportant, an instability has arrived into the situation which one way or another has eventually to be rectified. In the case of Britain, the crisis has been a chronic one: finance has been an end for decades, and production has become seen as an irrelevance for decades. The capitalist hegemony has acted as if it did not care if production became nothing. This turns upside down the relations between production and circulation of money: actions have been predicated on the expansion of the time involved in the circulation of money and the elimination of time spent in production. The cost has had to be borne by somebody. If foreign money is to be attracted, and if costs had to be kept down so that finance capital could service overseas production capital cheaply, the costs were passed on in a hidden form to the rest of British economic activity.

Other world financial centres have developed on the back of expansionist industrial capital (first the US and then Japan). But in Britain for most of this century, London has acted as a world finance centre despite a massive contraction in production. This is a contradiction.

The supporters of the City see it as the one redeeming feature of the economy. They do not question it, and yet the City has continued to play its leading role in the world economy as year by year, decade by decade, the economy as a whole has slipped and slipped. The supporters do not want to see the City's position harmed, and yet is its role unconnected to the decline in production? Is it just a coincidence that measures have been adopted to maintain the City's international position in the circulation of money, and measures have not been adopted to maintain Britain's position in terms of international production? Is it possible that the City sees itself as the whole economy and thus sees no need to ensure that the correct relations are restored with production?

The problems therefore stem from the internal relations of British capital. The extinguishing of production time has correlated with the burgeoning of circulation (of money) time. This correlated with the decline of manufacturing and the strength of finance capital. It is manifested culturally in the disdain for production. Which is itself a reflection of money fetishism. In consequence labour has not been valued. And the end result has been various crises and a limp growth in the skills and competence of workers and a limitation on the cultural life of most people.

CONCLUSIONS

The state is having great difficulty in coming to terms with the fact that British capital is refusing to take on ends which the state under Thatcherism would like it to take on: for example, training, hegemony with respect to the educational system and progressive management based on employee involvement. In its desire to avoid the opposite conclusion, which is that the British state was a reluctant interventionist (which it was in international terms), required to intervene because British capital was not doing things, it is now beginning to adopt a new strategy which involves a subtly new relation between the state and business. Instead of a crude laissez-faire approach, the Thatcher Government is beginning to see its job in terms of socialising British capital. The new target for Thatcherism is not British labour but British capital.

The state has set itself, in certain areas, the task of inculcating new social and cultural orientations amongst British capital. The public sector and public agencies are twisted inside out in a bid to promote these new social and cultural orientations.

10 Political and Social Policies for Valued Labour

INTRODUCTION

The problems of Britain's labour markets, the skill shortages, recruitment difficulties, the discrimination, have deep roots in history. Tracing these roots has led further and further into the social relations of Britain, and into the evolution of cultural conditions. At first sight these essentially economic problems seemed bad enough, but looked at economically they could be seen as small ripples on the calm surface of orthodox labour market theory. As their fuller nature was theoretically brought to light they suggested that the social economy of Britain is confronted by a contradiction which can only be developed through social and political action.

That contradiction concerns the dual nature of labour which consists of labour having the potential to create useful products and of having the property of being expressed in actual products. The capacity to make useful things and the property of forming the substance of useful things are not the same thing, but the one turns into the other whenever production occurs successfully. In the advanced Western countries this generally depends on production being kept up to date so that goods and services can be successfully traded. In other words, the development of labour consists of the overcoming of this contradiction by making and consuming products which require higher and higher levels of scientific and technological know-how and which satisfy ever more developed tastes and needs. Put simply, Britain has been failing to modernise its production processes, products and above all its labour, in line with the necessities established by world trading conditions. We believe that its failure in this task is based upon its failure to understand the full social and economic value of labour in a modern and modernising economy.

173

The only lesson that successive Governments have learnt in tackling world trading conditions has been a consistent attempt to interfere with simple prices of goods. This has either taken place through attempts to limit the price level of wages and therefore keep prices down, or through interference with the market level of the pound. Obviously, whilst this latter mechanism has no direct relationship to costs at the point of production, it does have a very powerful role in overall competitiveness. Whilst the Ford workers are always lectured about the effect of their wage demands upon international competitiveness, if the pound 'strengthens' one day against the next on the international money market it has a sustantially greater effect upon Ford's competitiveness than increasing wages by 10 per cent above inflation. The simple, and apparently straightforward, stress upon wage costs as the main factor in competitiveness means that the the main fear of foreign competition has been held up to be the low-wage Pacific rim economies, and their workforce has been praised in relationship to ours because of its low-cost approach. We should stress that this argument played a major role in the Callaghan Government's explanation of problems of world competition – as well as that of the Thatcher administration.

Our point in the book so far has been to demonstrate that the crises of production experienced by the British economy have a broad series of factors involved and the one that directly concerns labour is the lack of investment that has been placed *not* in plant and machinery, but in labour itself. Our overall point is that one of the major factors of production – labour – or to express it another way – people – has been deeply undervalued and underinvested in all its forms and potential forms.

Consequently it is not surprising that, contrary to first impressions, the crisis in this failure to modernise has been getting deeper and more fundamental under a series of Governments that have developed no role in increasing the value of labour within the economy. Indeed Thatcherism in most of the 1980s was mainly aggravating the crisis by interventions which attacked social distribution and attacked the 'second order productive labour' of public service workers, whose labour added to capitalist accumulation by enhancing the labour power of British workers; and it aggravated the crisis by interventions which impeded fixed capital formation. Thatcherism instead diverted efforts down the laissez-faire route of a modern form of 'labour intensification', which broadly means forcing more time spent actually on working into working hours and forcing work to occur at a higher rate of energy consumption for the worker. Labour flexibility was the modern version of this and it was pushed and extolled to private capitalists. Thatcherism also sought an economy-wide labour intensification when it called on workers to be more mobile: each individual worker who heeded the call to be mobile, or responded to the Government-induced conditions which made mobility more likely, was cutting down, on the personal level, the time spent during potential working lives in the non-labour of waiting for a job to come along.

Following the argument in this book so far we should underline the way in which this economic policy managed to recreate precisely the opposite conditions from those which were wanted. By attempting all the time to cut down on the amount of time that labour was not working by seeing such time as an economic waste, all the activities that went on in that time have been treated and signified by the Government as a waste and a cost upon resources. The economic image we have been offered is one of the worker at the bench or at the desk actually producing wealth, and the worker not at the bench actually costing wealth.

Thus, the argument runs, we must increase and intensify the time at the bench and decrease and denigrate the time away. This set of ideas, which has dominated all social and political as well as economic policy, is simplistic cost accounting. In the real economic world of production it is the time spent away from the bench or the desk that can – at the right time and in the right way – add *more* to production than the time spent at the bench.

The most obvious and continual argument is training. When the workforce is being trained it is not producing, and is therefore a cost. As a cost, so the above argument goes, it must be reduced and the time at the bench intensified. In this way, the cost accounting approach of the Government has escalated the already barren approach to training that characterises the British economy.

This is the political point we have reached after 10 years of Thatcherism. The contradiction which should have been addressed has been intensified by the policies that have been followed. What then are the policies that may bring the nation's economy back to one of development?

THE MARKET AND THE HIDDEN HAND OF SELF-INTEREST

The New Right not only do not perceive the central contradiction in the historical development of the social-economy, they also believe that self-interest, as focused and canalised by free market forces, will solve the problems that face Britain. This is market fetishism.

By the end of the 1980s the list of changes to help free up the market was very impressive (Treasury, 1989). There was hardly a corner of national life that had not been touched. Employment, care, housing, education, training, insurance, investment and saving and, of course, taxation had all been reformed and affected at some time in the 1980s. Helping the market was interpreted by the Government as reforming the supply side of markets. This was, from a tax point of view, a matter of removing disincentives and removing tax induced biases. Thus the basic income tax rate had been reduced, presumably to increase the supply of labour by raising the rewards of labour. The abolition of national insurance contributions of lower paid employees was seen as particularly relevant to the supply of young and unskilled labour, as were the multiple changes in the social security laws. Cuts in corporation tax and capital gains tax had also been made, possibly to increase the supply of capital.

The supply of low paid workers was seen as especially helped by the tax and security reforms made in the late 1980s:

> The reductions in income tax and national insurance rates, together with social security reforms in 1988, have significantly reduced the 'unemployment trap', where people could be better off unemployed than in work. Under the social security reforms, entitlement to income-related benefits is based on net income so that people cannot lose more in benefit withdrawal and income tax than they gain in gross pay, leaving them worse off after a pay increase. The introduction of Family Credit for people in work has also helped, with take-up and average benefit awards already well above those for Family Income Supplement, which it replaced in April last year. (Treasury, 1989, p.5)

Other measures identified by the Treasury as helping markets work better included: the Enterprise Allowance Scheme, changes in the law on pensions, housing legislation which enabled council tenants to buy their houses or change their landlords, deregulation of private tenancies, relaxation of regulations protecting employment conditions of employees, abolition of the Dock Labour Scheme, trade union legislation, the introduction of a national curriculum in schools, the opening of City Technology Colleges, the Youth Training Scheme, introduction of 'Compacts' between inner city schools and employers, the National Restart Programme for the unemployed, Jobclubs for the unemployed, the Employment Training Scheme, the setting up of Training and Enterprise Councils and a National Training Task Force, abolition of exchange controls, deregulation of the Stock Exchange, changes in the legislation on building societies enabling them to compete with other financial businesses, reform of tax on life assurance, new legislation on investor protection and on banking supervision, the introduction of personal equity plans, subsidised management consultancy for smaller firms, changes in regional policy on Government grants, and privatisation. In the Treasury's view, these measures varied in their importance but all contributed to efficient, flexible markets.

The trouble with the New Right is that they only ever see half the picture. Firstly, they see that self-interest is important, but they fail to see that self-interest has to be brought into alignment with the general interest through the political process. That is, policy which encourages individual action to be based simply on self-interest does not *actually* produce good results all or most of the time. The policy maker in Government has to work on the basis that self-interest and general interest *ought* to be in harmony. Asking people to act against their self-interest for the general interest is highly problematic. In consequence policy making should be guided by the end of making self-interest and the 'good of the country' harmonise.

Secondly, the aim of liberation of self-interest from state control, as demanded by the New Right, is essentially correct, but false in the way that the New Right try to operationalise it. The liberation they attempt is based on abolition of state control over the social-economy. This is counter-productive because for most people the state is instrumental in their liberation, even though things can go wrong and states can, under certain conditions, end up a tyrannical force, rather than a liberating one.

To reiterate, for most people the liberation of self-interest from state control is not to be achieved by abolishing state control over the social-economy. Liberation of self-interest for the vast bulk of people requires the subjection of elements of that individual self-interest to a communal control which is guided and controlled by, and for, the majority of people. In other words, popular and fully democratic government actualises the liberation of self-interest. The removal of state control merely leads to the negation of individual self-interest for the majority by the dominance of the interests of a few.

Since labour is only important economically when it is working, the self-interest of labour is, in this model, only met when it is working. Other actions, such as training, are against interest. Similarly, when an employer employs someone, he or she will do so at the cheapest rate and only pay them when they are working. The model goes on to explain that it is in the interests of the worker to get paid more, and surely a job which needs training will pay more. But it is not in the interests of the workers to spend the time getting trained – so they will pretend to be trained and get the job.

Similarly for the employer, he or she needs to get trained workers but does not want to pay for their training or pay them more when they are trained. So they will pay only slightly more for someone who claims that they can do the job even though they have not been trained. This process leads to what we have termed counterfeiting of skills, and whilst individual employers and employees may gain from such fraud the material economy as a whole loses.

Both sides' self-interest therefore puts a premium on fudging the truth about training. A system which had regulations about who could and who could not do certain forms of work, dependent on qualifications, would stop that. But that would be a form of regulation and a form of intrusion in the self-interest of the people involved. The 'hidden hand', therefore, of a myriad of different bits of self-interest underlines the extent to which those self-interests, if allowed to operate freely, would act against training. It also encourages young people to leave school and training (dead and non-earning time) to take up employment (live and paid time). Such a system would create the lowest staying-on-at-school rate in the industrial world – and it has.

The assumption of the 'hidden hand' behind the self-interested actions of players in the market is very Utopian. Take the example of the experience of the Thatcher Government's attempts in the late 1980s to tackle inflation (getting inflation down was seen to be for the country's general good) by using high interest rates. The raising of interest rates was meant to cut consumer borrowing by making credit more expensive; this was preferred to alternative methods because it entailed only minimal interference with private initiative. As a result of this policy, private sector institutions lending money in the form of mortgages were faced with a choice: if they raised their mortgage rates they helped the Government to reduce inflation, thereby acting for the good of the country, and if they offered deferred mortgage rates they held on to or expanded their own share of the mortage market, which was in their self-interest but defeated the Government's policy. It was a choice between acting for the general good or acting for self-interest. Many decided to act in self-interest.

SOCIAL ACTION WITHIN A DEMOCRATIC FRAMEWORK

Against the limited view offered by the economics of labour, we pose our alternative view within the context of labour's duality as labour and as citizen. Put most simply the development of the former is not possible without the development of the latter. Thus our economic policy for the re-valuation of labour is based upon a network of social policies specifically designed to change the value of labour in the social world.

In explaining our notion of the citizen, we develop it out of the role of the social relations that are internal to democratic decision making and see these as fundamental to the social development of both people and labour. Indeed this is especially so in the economic sphere with its social relations of producing, exchanging, distributing and consuming. This development is obviously one that takes place over time both in the workplace and in society. The emergence of social distribution through state activity and second-order productive labour in the 20th century provides an important base for the further development of both labour and citizen.

Our starting point on citizenship is different since we identify as one of the nation's greatest *economic* problems the lack of value placed upon labour. Our starting point is the concept of the citizen at its simplest. An individual citizen, in any period and in any modern democratic capitalist society, has a stong self-understanding of what is in their own interests and what actions they should take to enhance their own welfare. The individual citizen also has a moral sense, an understanding of right and wrong in their society, and a view of their duties. At many times the individual finds a clash between self-interest and social duty. Many times the self-interest of one individual is in conflict with the interests of others with whom they are in a social relationship. This leads to, amongst other things, a difference of view about current social duties and responsibilities.

In a democratic society, the reconciling of self-interest and the 'general good', and the reconciling of different views of the general good, are attempted through the democratic process. Where successful, people agree generally on the actions which are in the general good and these are imposed through the law as duties which citizens must obey. The rights and obligations of the citizen may be defined in relation to various spheres, including political life, family, education, work and so on. To the degree that the individual citizen comes to accept the duties as right, to the degree that they are persuaded of their intrinsic value, the citizen incorporates them into their view of their own interest and welfare. As a result, they obey the state's insistence on these duties, seeing them as being in harmony with their own interests, indeed seeing them as being a self-imposition, and the general good is thus realised in a way consistent with liberty. The state's insistence on the duties of the citizen has to be a self-imposition if self-interest and the general good are to be harmonised under conditions of liberty. This requires democratic decision-making in its fullest sense. The nature of an absolute democracy would be one based squarely on interaction between citizens.

We must stress that our definition of democracy must include a full set of democratic *experiences* and not a set of formal voting rights. By stressing the word experience we are underlining the importance of engagement between citizen and society and not purely the holding of formal rights. The events of the last few months in Eastern Europe stress the importance of actually having formal democratic rights, but democracy should not be interpreted as simply stopping with those rights. People are arguing for the experience of democracy in their lives – and that must lie at the core of our social and economic policy for the revaluing of labour.

Over 150 years experience of the world of work has underlined this necessary co-operation in relationships between members of a workforce. Whilst it may be obvious to the people who own them that IBM and Wang are essentially in competition for markets, and that this competition represents the motif for their interaction, for the workforce inside these companies the main experience that they have of work is one of co-operation between different people to produce goods or services.

If labour is not prepared to adjust their individual self-interest with regard to activities such as when they will eat, when they will turn up and leave, how they will work and what exactly they will work on today, then very little will ever happen in terms of production. In other words if labour does not adjust its self-interest in relationship to the other people that they work with, then the whole process of work breaks down. The essence of work, in both small scale and large scale production, is an experience of constant and necessary co-operation. Some political economists would argue that labour is only prepared to engage in limiting this self interest through fear of discipline and loss of remuneration. But this is to misunderstand the day by day experience of the world of work. For where the limitation of self interest only takes place through terror, the constant necessity to enforce and reinforce that terror creates an unstable environment. In other parts of production we have experienced the limitations of self interest breaking down, and this not only results in chaos and loss of production but the actual experience of work under these circumstances for labour is *not* liberating but deeply dissatisfying.

People at work, when they are at work, have to experience co-operation with other people in a much more advanced way than those same people experience in their community and political life. For example, people are more likely to work co-operatively at work in producing goods and services than in the local street, or in the realm of consumption as a whole when the relationships beyond the family are very limited. For example, there are very few voluntary organisations to clear up litter from the streets.

Given the day by day experience of co-operation at work it is an essentially social activity which limits the extent to which people simply 'act for themselves'. At work individual citizens come to recognise the need to revise their view of their self-interest and actions which are oriented to their own welfare.

Democratic decision making with regards to the general good, and its implementation via the identification and imposition of duties, is a matter of political strategy. If a political stratgey is genuinely *democratic* then it can only be genuinely voluntary. By this we mean that whilst people may be *forced* to vote by the law, they cannot be forced to engage in a full range of democratic experiences. Habermas has stressed the importance of political strategy being free of compulsion:

> The sole possible justification at this level is consensus, aimed at in practical discourse, among the participants, who, in the conscious-ness of their common interests and their knowledge of the circumstances, of the predictable consequences, are the only ones who can know what risks they are willing to undergo, and with what expectations.(Habermas, 1974, p.33)

So self-interest, where it is mediated by practical discourse, achieves consensus and leads to the formation and realisation of a socialised self-interest which is essentially based on a congruent view of the citizen's duties, and is identical to the general interest.

A major barrier to the realisation of an all-round development of the citizen under historical conditions was the fact that democratic decision making was for a long time restricted from entry into the area of social-economy. This corresponded to the period of laissez-faire capitalism, when the main processes in which labour was involved were production, simple circulation and consumption and when second-order productive labour was barely developed to any significant degree. Because there could be no involvement by labour in the democratic decision making processes of the social relations of the world of work, there was in consequence no involvement by labour in democratic decision making on the development of labour itself!

Of course, as we have consistently pointed out, Thatcher has made this a much worse experience for labour. In failing to identify a major role for labour in the whole social and political project, the Government has placed labour in general and labour as individual worker (or indeed someone who is simply just thinking of going out to work) in a marginal position both economically and socially. The vision for labour under Thatcher was limited to economically working harder, costing less by asking for less wages, consuming more or less when the money supply requires it and socially and politically keeping quiet. The offer of involvement opening up before labour under these circumstances within the Thatcher project is distinctly limited.

The valuing of labour through investment in training and decent conditions is supplemented, as we will go on to describe, by the necessary changes in economic and political democracy to demonstrate that our structures want labour to have a say. But alongside this is the change in morale for a section of society to have its activity, and the outcomes of that activity, move to the centre of the economic and social stage – which would be dramatic.

A concrete example was the 'morale' of teachers in the last few years of the 1980s. Their low pay played a role in that low morale: coupled with very difficult changes in working conditions and the removal from 1987 to 1990 of their right to have a role in collective bargaining over their pay. But of equal significance is the the fact that the Thatcher project in education marginalised their activity in the education process. Since they were not important, why should they add that extra half hour of unpaid work? Why should they experience that extra sweat and worry? If we *are* marginal then not doing that extra will not matter. If we *are* to operate purely in self-interest then I am off from this staff room.

A different analysis which places labour at the centre of the world of work and the nature of production would change that immediately. It is important to note the costs of moving labour in from the margins though. By moving labour to the centre of economic growth we are also making it much more possible for labour to be criticised and underline its importance for change. If labour really does not matter in the productive process, then of course there is no point in changing or improving it. There is no point in demonstrating that it could do better, or be trained, or be more flexible, and so on. If, on the other hand, labour is central to economic growth then its criticism and its change is also central.

This *civilised plan for labour* will then be more critical of labour as a part of economic growth – mainly because it matters more.

Under the conditions in which the state was kept out of the economic sphere, the formation of the general good with respect to labour's development was presented as identical to the playing out of self-interest in the 'false liberty' of unmediated self-interested action. In actuality, the development of labour remained a matter not of the general interest in society, but of private self-interest, which principally meant capital's interest. Thus citizens, as citizens, were not concerned with labour's development.

Labour's involvement in its development rested on its own initiative under duress and compulsion from capital. This was essentially the nature of British craft workers self-control in the 19th century. Its obvious limitations were that it required extremely favourable external circumstances for labour to counter capital's compulsion and direction of labour's development. Relatively few workers in the 19th century were in such favourable circumstances.

The growth of social distribution and second-order productive labour, since both involve the state, brought the potential for labour generally to get involved in democratic decision making processes with regard to labour's development. There is a deep sense in which the real development of labour's role as a franchised citizen rested on the arrival of mature capitalism. Because only with social distribution and second-order productive labour could labour's self-interest *as labour* be brought into democratic decision making.

The growth of social distribution and second-order productive labour was momentous. Labour could in a self-aware and conscious manner play a role in the direction of its own development: labour's development could become self-development! This was a cultural leap forward.

LABOUR'S SELF-DEVELOPMENT IN BRITAIN

In this chapter there is an important philological point to be made about the word labour. For the rest of the book the reader needs to carefully note the first letter of the word since we are discussing the way in which labour in its particular self development in this country, created as its vehicle a party of that same name. The Labour Party, then, becomes the vehicle for the development of labour. We are suggesting that through a richer democratic involvement as citizens, labour begins to play a more significant role in its own development rather than being developed (or in Britain's case underdeveloped) by capital. It would have been naive to expect that the transition from labour's development by capital to labour's self-development would have proceeded smoothly and without set-backs. The transition has to date in fact proved to be full of set-backs and hitches and most obviously is far from complete. It would be nearer the mark to say that it has barely begun.

Two major difficulties have stood out so far. Firstly, in terms of the structure of both citizenry and the labour market, the development of labour's independent self-consciousness is patchy. This appears to happen because for very many citizens (labour) their experience of society and work contains little self-realisation. Given that their experience of self realisation is not high it is very hard to construct a common interest in directing the self-development of labour. Until this fully materialises, labour will continue to see its labour in an alienated way, and fail to see or identify with the general social interest in the social productiveness of labour.

In this overall experience, any activity that labour may put in to improving itself is not for itself, but for the employer. If the employee is provided with any vision of increased worth through training, it comes only in the incentive of increased money and *not* intrinsic experience itself.

Secondly, the strategies evolved by those elements of labour that *have* been involved in political and social development have been faulty. The most important issue has been their sectarian nature. For whilst the Labour Party has played a serious role in the government of the country at national and local level, as a political organisation that is capable of developing strategy it has been flawed by its sectarian approach. Over the years it has succeeded in representing those people whom it sees as 'the class' and has not represented those absent from that vision. This is not surprising since its vision of the world is likely to be limited to those who are a part of that world. It does however raise crucial questions about the way in which labour has developed its strategy in the past through its particular organisation of self actualisation. The first phase of a developed, mature capitalism in

Britain, which ran from the late 1940s until the late 1970s, demonstrated the existence of many deficiencies in the strategy followed by labour.

Amongst the chief failures of the strategy were:

(1)   The political and economic failure to ensure that social distribution was efficiently organised, and especially to ensure that it was sensitive to the needs of the citizen.

(2)   The economic failure to organise second-order productive labour more effectively for the more rapid development of labour.

(3)   The economic and social failure to organise the balance between production and consumption required for a faster growth in the general social productiveness of labour.

(4)   The political and economic failure to organise the proper subsumption of finance capital under production capital.

(5)   The political failure to extend democratic decision making in society, both in terms of state activity and economic relations of production, simple circulation, social distribution, and consumption.

These failures were experienced by large sections of the citizenry and labour force as examples which demonstrate the impossibility of labour itself taking a leading role in running either economy or society. The pursuing of highly sectarian interests undermined any approach to develop a wide enough strategy for labour to feel able to take charge of the process of realisation. For example, until the 1970s the TUC consistently argued against the development of worker directors since it cut across the power of trade unions and their role in collective bargaining, a prime example of the rejection of one form of empowerment because it failed to meet certain sectarian criteria. Welfare services in local authorities and the NHS, the social security system and public housing, had developed massive unaccountable bureaucracies. People who worked in them, or were served by them, did not experience them as part of a democratic experience.

The Labour movement had developed the power of labour and its ability to intervene in very particular ways. Labour was developed in confrontation with capital: it was developed in large-scale organisations to combat capital and it was developed in large-scale state organisations to have the power to intervene. Such experiences are not a simple historical 'mistake' but have developed out of the way in which labour saw itself as a part of historical experience. The need for large battalions to 'take on' British capital created the particular trade unions and Labour Party of the period. They then created images of themselves in state institutions.

The 1980s represented a period of strategy renewal for labour (and here we stress the small l, since whilst a great deal of strategic rethinking went on within the Labour Party much went on outside it, within social movements that were equally important in broadening the previous sectarianism of the approach of labour). Even so the growth of labour's self-development has been a long historical process, and we predict that further advances will be upset from time to time with further difficulties. This expectation rests above all on the judgement that mature capitalism is prone to economic crisis, and the state is inevitably engaged in crisis management. These crises however are better handled in a society that is being progressively democratised. This is because, as we have been at pains to argue, successful capitalism under the conditions of the late 20th century is mature and has created conditions in which labour must increase in value. This happens at least in part through an increase in self-consciousness which will press forward to its self-development.

The role of education and training in this development is central and there are signs of the British trade union movement becoming more aware of the need for better and more responsive training and education. In 1989 for example, the Trades Union Congress published an important statement on this matter. It was called *Skills 2000*. The TUC insisted that continuously developing the skills of working people was a high priority.

> To ensure economic growth and competitiveness, and to make sure that individuals can realise their potential both work-related and personal, we need to expand massively the amount of training in the economy and the level of skills in the workforce. To achieve that growth, individuals must be allowed and encouraged to develop their competence throughout their working lives, through both education and training. And to ensure that their individual progression contributes to the needs of the nation, the training they undertake must be industry-led and relevant to employment. (TUC, 1989, p.1)

Much of this historical process is nation specific, and if a nation's labour fails to press forward to its self-development it can only mean that the social and economic system will inevitably lose ground to modern capitalist economies. We have argued that this process of self-development can only take place inside and outside of the workplace and therefore take the form of growing democratisation – and attempts to resist this will raise political crises.

A JAPANESE VISION OF THE FUTURE

Japan is without doubt the leading capitalist country. Its strategy certainly includes a considerable emphasis on state planning. This has extended to the planning of social and urban infrastructures.

The latest illustration of this can be seen in proposals to build an entire city in Australia. The Ministry of Trade and Industry (MITI) in Japan envisaged, in 1987, building a modern and cosmopolitan city of at least 100000 people. It was conceived as a meeting point of many different cultures, and as uniting its people in a new culture. It would provide the setting of hi-tech industry and would provide a market place for the exchange of advanced science and technology. It was seen as an opportunity to build a city free from the problems of established cities. It would provide amenities for everyday living as well as natural beauty and comfort.

Critics have cast doubts on the MITI vision of an end to the contradictions of modern societies in this city designed for the 21st century. And the response of the Australians may be to block the project in its 1987 form and to sanction instead an alternative form of Japanese investment. Nevertheless it shows that the most successful capitalist economy saw the importance of a total planning of the social and cultural environment within which labour develops, and conceived the 21st century environment strategically in terms of advanced science and technology.

THE LONG TERM

In the long term the social-economy of Britain will be one in which labour plays a much more important role in the development of labour than it does currently. This transition will go hand in hand with the democratisation of society, especially in respect of the social-economy, which will move citizens in their mutual relations towards the realisation of a just society, a caring society, and one in which individuals seek to actualise their potential.

The requirements for the long term include:

(1) Humanised working situations, including meaningful work and industrial democracy.

(2) Public educational and training services which provide people with the necessary skills and competence for work in a society in which scientific and technological knowledge will be even more important than they are now.

(3) Equality of opportunity.

(4) Quality of life, including a safe and healthy environment and sufficient spare time to provide people with ample opportunity for cultural, artistic, recreational and spiritual activities.

(5) The expansion and deepening of democracy in society.

If we are to get there sooner rather than later, it requires that we treat the short term as the first step towards the long term.

HERE AND NOW

In making the first steps towards the long term goals of a society which values labour, as outlined in the preceding section, Britain will need infrastructural development to assist the growth of productivity through improved direct and indirect investment in labour.

This will include the improvement of the educational and training infrastructure. Britain will need to raise its levels of technical, scientific and vocational education and training. This is needed not only to boost the numbers of professional scientists and technologists, but also the general scientific and technological competence of the whole UK workforce, as well as the managerial competence of those responsible for organising the work of others. Britain needs many more skilled, competent workers who will be capable of using tho most modern fixed capital.

Since one of the prime aims of increasing the extent of training is to construct a much higher proportion of flexible trained workers who can take increasing control of their own work experiences and careers, it is essential that the form and content of training represents these goals. At the end of the 1980s, as we have explained in Chapters 2 and 4, most of the training infrastructure was deeply rigidified within certain forms. It provided a form of alphabet soup approach to qualifications, with little possibility of mixed-mode credit accumulation and little possibility of using one set of training experiences as the base for job change. Pedagogic methods are often not likely to create a workforce with an interest in thinking for itself. So the detail of training must change.

In designing the upgrading of this infrastructure particular attention will need to be paid to job related training for older workers, who will become an increasingly large proportion of the UK workforce, and on whom the dynamism of industry will depend as we approach the year 2000.

This aspect of the infrastructure is very deficient: the informed consensus in Britain is that the UK workforce is undereducated, undertrained, underskilled and underpaid. And yet, simply expanding education and training will not necessarily be realised in a higher quality workforce. Labour which has been educated and trained is capable of producing larger amounts of material wealth but only if the workers' talents are usefully employed. Nevertheless the most successful economies do have higher levels of education and training. The key to their success is that they are able to use the high quality workforce produced by their educational and training infrastructures because they are developing new products and processes with higher scientific and technological bases. Unless Britain does likewise, the production of a more educated and trained workforce could be wasted.

This leads to the next point: the infrastructure for scientific and technological progress needs to be boosted, along with mechanisms for ensuring technology transfer across the education-industry interface. But science itself has not been problematic so much as its day by day technological applications.

Finally, transport, telecommunications and energy, which have been grossly mismanaged, will have to be brought into economic production as an essential investment and not as a trading industry in their own right.

The immediate problems facing any Government committed to an economic strategy of modernisation of the infrastructure (workforce skills and knowledge, transport and research and development) and investment in fixed capital equipment stem from the necessity for the country to refrain from consumption. This will require the transition of the country culturally, and in a very short space of time, into a society in which there is general identification with the common interest. This will require an enormous social change, in which confidence and trust in each other's sense of social solidarity and social responsibility provides a sound base for a strategy of transforming the social-economy.

The changes outlined above will need to be reinforced by the development of more constructive industrial relations. This will require attention to job design, management styles, payment systems, disciplinary practices, and eventually industrial democracy. Industrial relations will need to play a part in raising the level of productivity in industry through the greater application of the involvement of the workforce.

Improvements in the design of work, for example, team working, factories-within-factory organisation and cellular organisation, have already been tried out in a number of British factories. Part of the aim of these types of organisational innovation is to reduce monotonous work, to use group forms of organisation to get away from the fragmentation of work.

Changes in work organisation, such as team working, are not enough by themselves to create a new spirit in industry. Changes in management would also be indispensable, particularly the introduction of worker participation in management. By combining new forms of work organisation and worker participation in management, Britain could experience a new creative attitude to work, replacing the alienated experience that characterises so much of work today.

The need for change in management style was already being reflected in the late 1980s in the Government's exhortation to companies to adopt employee involvement. The Department of Employment newspaper, *Employment News*, carried the headline in November 1989 (No. 180, p.1): 'GET THEM INVOLVED'.

The Department of Employment reported on a new Government booklet which stated that employee involvement was one of the major success stories of British industry. A variety of benefits were claimed for employee involvement: more co-operative atmosphere, increased flexibility, improved joint problem solving, increased job satisfaction, and smoother introduction of major changes.

The importance of worker participation in management for the development of labour's skills and capacities, as well as for the motivational and other advantages claimed by the Government report on employee involvement, makes the urgency of legislation on industrial democracy a priority in any strategy for the immediate future of Britain. Developments in the education and training infrastructure would need to assist the development of skills and competences in the UK workforce, which would be needed to implement industrial democracy.

One of the most difficult problems for the immediate strategy on the development of labour is the environmental crisis. The scandalous and irresponsible treatment of the environment in Britain has been subsidising profits at the expense of the known and hidden costs to the community. The strategy for the next few years will have to respond to widespread public concern for the environment, and seek not only to avoid further damage but also to reverse some of the worst problems already manufactured by reckless business practice.

CONCLUSIONS

The British social-economy moved into a definite new stage when the welfare state and public services were expanded after the second world war. This new period marked the strong development of labour's self-development, when labour in its role of citizen introduced its interest in its own development into the democratic decision making processes of the British state. This was important in cultural terms but subsequent progress has been slow. As a result, labour productivity falls further and further behind and awaits a major change of strategy before any real prospect of sustainable economic progress can be realised.

The answer to the problem of labour's self-development is to be found in the full development of the individual as both labour and as a democratic citizen. Through expanding and deepening democratisation of British society, especially in respect of its economic relations, the reconciling of self-interest and the 'general good', will lead to a pressing forward on the continuous development of the skills of the UK workforce. This is the only way to overcome the stagnation of the economy produced by reliance on the market, with its cultural conservatism, and its inability to develop a strategy for mature capitalist international trading. Labour's development in Britain was held back under laissez-faire capitalism because capital was responsible for the organisation of its development: labour was undervalued as an organising force in society. The challenge for labour of the years ahead is to develop practices which demonstrate the capacity for increased investment in itself as a guarantee for increased wealth for the future. It has the opportunity and awareness to struggle for favourable material and cultural conditions for its self-realisation.

Bibliography

Abbot and Bompas (1943) *The Woman Citizen and Social Security* (London).

ACAS (1988) *Labour Flexibility in Britain*, Occasional Paper 41.

Aldcroft, D.H. (1983) *The British Economy Between the Wars* (Oxford: Philip Allan).

Anwar, M. (1986) *Race and Politics* (London: Tavistock).

Banham, J. (1989) 'Vocational Training in British Business', *National Westminster Bank Quarterly Review*, February, pp.4–12.

Baran, P.A. and P.M. Sweezy (1966) *Monopoly Capital* (Harmondsworth: Penguin).

Beechey, V., and T. Perkin, (1987) *A Matter of Hours* (Cambridge, Polity).

Beynon, H. (1973) *Working for Ford* (Harmondsworth: Penguin).

Blauner, R. (1964) *Alienation and Freedom* (The University of Chicago Press).

Board of Education (1938), Report of the Consultative Committee: *Secondary Education*, (*Spens Report*), HMSO.

Board of Education (1943), Report of the Committee of the Secondary School Examinations Council: *Curriculum and Examinations in Secondary Schools*, (Norwood Report), HMSO.

Brittan, S. (1985) *Two Cheers for Self-Interest*, Occasional Paper 73, The Institute of Economic Affairs.

Brown, C. (1984) *Black and White Britain. The Third PSI Survey* (Aldershot: Gower).

Brown, C., and P. Gay (1985) *Racial Discrimination 17 Years After the Act* (PSI).

Buck, N., I. Gordon and K. Young, with J. Ermisch and L. Mills (1986) *The London Employment Problem* (Oxford: Clarendon Press).

Cole, G.D.H. (1933) *The Intelligent Man's Guide Through World Chaos* (London: Victor Gollancz).

Coalter, F. (1989) *Freedom and Constraint* (London: Routledge and Kegan Paul).

Coates, K. and T. Topham (1988) *Trade Unions in Britain* (London: Fontana).

Corrigan, P. (1979) *Schooling the Smash Street Kids* (London: Macmillan).

Cronin, J.E. (1979) *Industrial Conflict in Modern Britain* (London: Croom Helm).

Daly, A., D.M.W.N. Hitchens and K. Wagner (1985) 'Productivity, Machinery and Skills in a Sample of British and German Manufacturing Plants', *National Institute Economic Review*, No.111, February, pp.48–61.

Daniel, W.W. (1987) *Workplace Industrial Relations and Technical Change* (London: Frances Pinter).

Davidoff, L. (1979) 'The separation of home and work? Landladies and lodgers in nineteenth and twentieth-century England', in S. Burman (ed.) *Fit Work for Women* (London Croom Helm)

Dennis, N., F. Henriques, and C. Slaughter (1969) *Coal is Our Life* (London: Tavistock).

Department of Education and Science (1977) *Education in schools* A Consultative Document, Cmnd 6869.

Department of Employment (1989) '1988 Labour Force Survey – Preliminary Results', *Employment Gazette*, April, pp.182–195.

Department of Trade and Industry (1988) *The Single Market. The Facts.*

Employment Department (1988) *Employment for the 1990s* (London: HMSO).

Eastwood, G. (1976) *Skilled Labour Shortages in the United Kingdom*, British-North American Committee.

Education Group (1981) *Unpopular Education: Schooling and Social Democracy in England since 1944* (CCCS/Hutchinson).

Employment Institute Economic Report (1989) 'Women and unemployment', vol. 4, No. 5, May.

Engels, F. (1969) *The Condition of the Working Class in England* (London: Granada Publishing).

Finn, D. (1987) *Training without Jobs* (London: Macmillan).

Foxall, G.R. (1980) *Consumer Behaviour* (London: Croom Helm).

Galbraith, J.K. (1967) *The New Industrial Estate* (Harmondsworth: Penguin)

Gardiner, J. (1976) 'Women and Unemployment', *Red Flag*, No.10.

Gilbert (1972) *The National Insurance Principle* (London: Batsford).

Goldthorpe, J.H., D. Lockwood, F. Bechofer and J. Platt (1969) *The Affluent Worker in the Class Structure* (Cambridge University Press).

Gough, I. (1979) *The Political Economy of the Welfare State* (London: Macmillan).

Greater London Council (1985) *The London Industrial Strategy.*

Greenley, G.E. (1989) *Strategic Management* (London: Prentice-Hall).

Habermas, J. (1974) *Theory and Practice* (London: Heinemann).

Halsey, A.H. (1987) 'Social Trends Since World War ll', *Social Trends*, 17, pp.11–19.

Hakim, C. (1987) 'Trends in the flexible workforce', *Employment Gazette*, November, pp.549–560.

Heilbroner, R.L. (1976) *Business Civilization in Decline* (Harmondsworth: Penguin).

Hobsbawm, E. (1964) *Labouring Men: Studies in the History of Labour* (London: Weidenfeld and Nicolson).

Hobsbawm, E. (1969) *Industry and Empire* (Harmondsworth: Penguin).

Hurstsfield, J. (1978) *The part time trap*, Low Pay Pamphlet No.9 (London: Low Pay Unit).

IRRR (1984) 'No-strike deals in perspective', Industrial Relations Review and Reports, 324, July, pp.8–11.

Jackson, M. P. (1988) *Trade Unions* (London: Longman).

Jarvis, V., and S.J. Prais (1989) 'Two Nations of Shopkeepers: Training for Retailing in France and Britain', *National Institute Economic Review*, Number 128, May, pp.58–74.

Jefferys, J.B. (1946) *The Story of the Engineers* (London: Lawrence and Wishart).

Joseph, K. (1978) 'Proclaim the message: Keynes is dead!' in P. Hutber (ed.) *What's Wrong with Britain?* (London: Sphere).

Kelly, J. (1988) *Trade Unions and Socialist Politics* (London: Verso).

Kincaid (1968) *Poverty and Inequality in Britain* (Harmondsworth: Penguin).
Laffin, M. (1989) *Managing under Pressure* (London: Macmillan).
Lane, T. (1974) *The Union Makes Us Strong* (London: Arrow).
Laski, H.J. (1940) *The Danger of Being a Gentleman* (London: George Allen and Unwin).
Lawrence (1911) *Five Points against the Insurance Bill* (London).
Leese, J. (1985) 'The Nissan agreement - a work philosophy', *Employment Gazette*, August, pp.326–7.
London Research Centre (1989) *Only Women's Work*, Research Series.
Lowe, R. (1967) *Primary and Secondary Education* (London).
Low Pay Unit (1989) *Poverty and Low Pay* (London).
Manpower Services Commission (1975) *Vocational Preparation for Young People*.
Marx, K. (1974) *Capital*, Volume 1 (London: Lawrence and Wishart).
Meegan, R. (1988) 'A crisis of mass production?' in J. Allen, and D. Massey, (eds) *The Economy in Question* (London: Sage).
McIlroy, J. (1988) *Trade Unions in Britain Today* (Manchester University Press).
Miles, R., and A. Phizacklea (1981) 'The TUC and Black Workers, 1974–76' in P. Braham, E. Rhodes, and M. Pearn (eds) *Discrimination and Disadvantage in Employment* (London: Harper and Row).
Miles, R.E and C.C. Snow (1978) *Organizational Strategy, Structure, and Process* (London: McGraw-Hill).
Mitchell, B.R. (1978) *European Historical Statistics* (London: Macmillan).
Moss (1989) 'Work, Family and the Care of Children – Issues of Equality and Responsibility', paper given to the National Children's Bureau.
National Youth Employment Council (1974) *Unqualified, Untrained and Unemployed* (HMSO).
Nichols, T. (1986) *The British Worker Question* (London: Routledge and Kegan Paul).
Offe, C. (1984) *Contradictions of the Welfare State* (London: Hutchinson).
Packard, V. (1957) *The Hidden Persuaders* (McKay).
Pearson, R., R. Hutt and D. Parsons (1984) *Education, Training and Employment* (Aldershot: Gower).
Pegge, T. (1986) 'Hitachi two years on', *Personnel Management*, October, pp.42–5.
Piore, M.J. (1975) 'Job Monotony, Employment Security, and Upward Mobility in the Labour Market Structure', in L.E. Davis and A.B. Cherns, (eds) *The Quality of Working Life* (Volume One, Problems, Prospects, and the State of the Art) (London: Free Press).
Prais, S.J. (1988) 'Qualified Manpower in Engineering', *National Institute Economic Review*, No.122, February, pp.76–83.
Rose, M. (1972) *The New Poor Law* (Harmondsworth: Penguin).
Rubery, J. and Tarling, R. (1988) 'Women's Employment in Declining Britain', in J. Rubery, (ed) *Women and Recession* (London: RKP).
Shonfield, A. (1965) *Modern Capitalism* (London: Oxford University Press).
SERTUC Women's Committee (1989) *Still Moving Towards Equality*.
Stedman Jones, G. (1986) *Language and Social Class* (Oxford University Press).

Steedman, H. and K. Wagner (1987) 'A Second Look at Productivity, Machinery and Skills in Britain and Germany', *National Institute Economic Review*, No.122, November, pp.84–95.

Steedman, H. and K. Wagner (1989) 'Productivity, Machinery and Skills: Clothing Manufacture in Britain and Germany', *National Institute Economic Review*, No.127, February, pp.40–57.

Taylor, D. (1984) 'Learning from the Japanese', *Employment Gazette*, June, pp.279–285.

Thompson, E. P. (1980) *The Making of the English Working Class* (Harmondsworth: Penguin).

Tillett, A., Kempner, T., and G. Wills (1970) *Management Thinkers* (Harmondsworth: Penguin).

TUC (1984) *TUC Strategy* (consultative document published in March 1984).

TUC (1989) *Skills 2000*, August.

Turner, H.A., G. Clack and G. Roberts (1967) *Labour Relations in the Motor Industry* (London: George Allen and Unwin).

Training Agency (n. d.), *Training in Britain, A Study of Funding, Activity and Attitudes, Summary* (HMSO).

Treasury (1983) *Economic Progress Report*, No.162, November.

Treasury (1989) 'Helping markets work better', *Economic Progress Report*, Number 203, August, pp.4–7.

Treasury (1989) *Economic Progress Report*, No.204, October.

Treasury (1990) *Economic Progress Report*, No.207, April.

Walby, S, (1986) *Patriarchy at Work* (Cambridge: Polity).

Work and Society (1984) 'Human values in working life', *Employment Gazette*, February, pp.54–5 and 64.

Williams, G. (1963) *Apprenticeship in Europe* (London: Chapman and Hall).

Willis, P. (1977) *Learning to Labour* (Farnborough: Saxon House).

OTHER SOURCES USED

British Public Opinion (MORI), Vol 5, Nos 5, and 10.

Disability Now, December 1989.

Ealing Planning and Economic Development (no date) *The Ealing Skills Survey Report*, London Borough of Ealing.

Employment Gazette, Historical Supplement, No.2, October 1987.

Employment Gazette, various volumes and numbers.

Employment Report, November 1986, Vol vii, No.3.

General Household Survey 1984.

Labour Market Quarterly Reports, various numbers.

National Institute Economic Review (NIER), various numbers.

OECD Main Economic Indicators.

Times Education Supplement, 22 October 1976.

TUC Bulletins, various numbers.

Index